Kids' Book of Giant Machines That

Crush, Cut, Dig, Drill, Excavate, Grade, Haul, Pave, Pump, Push, Roll, Stack, Thresh, and Transport

Big Things

By Erik Bruun
Illustrations by Carl Wiens

Black Dog
& Leventhal
Publishers
New York

Library of Congress
Cataloging-in-Publication Data

Bruun, Erik A., 1961-
Kids' book of giant machines / Erik Bruun ;
illustrated by Carl Wiens.
p. cm.
Summary: Describes huge machines that build,
demolish, cut, drill, and move massive things.
ISBN 1-57912-071-7
1. Machinery–Juvenile literature. 2. Motor
vehicles–Juvenile literature.
[1. Machinery.]
I. Title. II. Wiens, Carl, ill.
TJ147.B77 1999
621.8'6 21–dc21 99-040458

Front Cover:
Watercolor illustration by Carl Wiens
Back Cover:
Digital illustrations by Carl Wiens
Back Cover Photographs:
Liebherr *(center)*; NASA *(right)*;
Brown Brothers *(bottom)*

Book design: Clover Archer

Printed in Hong Kong.

Black Dog & Leventhal Publishers, Inc.
151 West 19th Street
New York, New York 10011

Distributed by
Workman Publishing Company
708 Broadway
New York, New York 10003

h g f e d c b a

KOMATSU

Introduction

The machines in this book are huge. Trucks as big as houses. Cranes as tall as skyscrapers. Shovels as big as buildings with buckets that can hold a six-car garage.

Big machines are a recent invention. Thousands of years ago, men and women used simple, human-sized shovels, hammers, and picks. There were no engines, so people had to use their muscle power instead of engine power. Slowly, people started to come up with new tools and machines to lessen the amount of muscle needed to dig a canal, lift heavy weights, or move materials.

Each new invention helped lead to another invention that made it easier for people to build roads, construct buildings, and improve harbors. The invention of the first simple steam engine in 1628 was a great leap forward, but it wasn't until railroads became popular in the 1830s that the era of heavy equipment really began.

All of a sudden, people needed to build railroad tracks to carry trains. This required moving huge amounts of dirt and rock—either by thousands of workers with shovels or by inventing new machines. In the United States, there were not enough people to do the digging for the long railroad lines that needed to be built across the vast country, so new machines such as the Otis steam shovel were invented to get the job done.

As new metals and engines were developed, constant improvements were made to the machines. Steam shovels got bigger and bigger, to the point where some were as large as a 20-story building. One shovel, operated by a single person, could do the work of 10,000 men with hand shovels.

Tractors, cranes, tree-cutting equipment, bulldozers, and tunneling machines all got bigger and better, too. The result is a world in

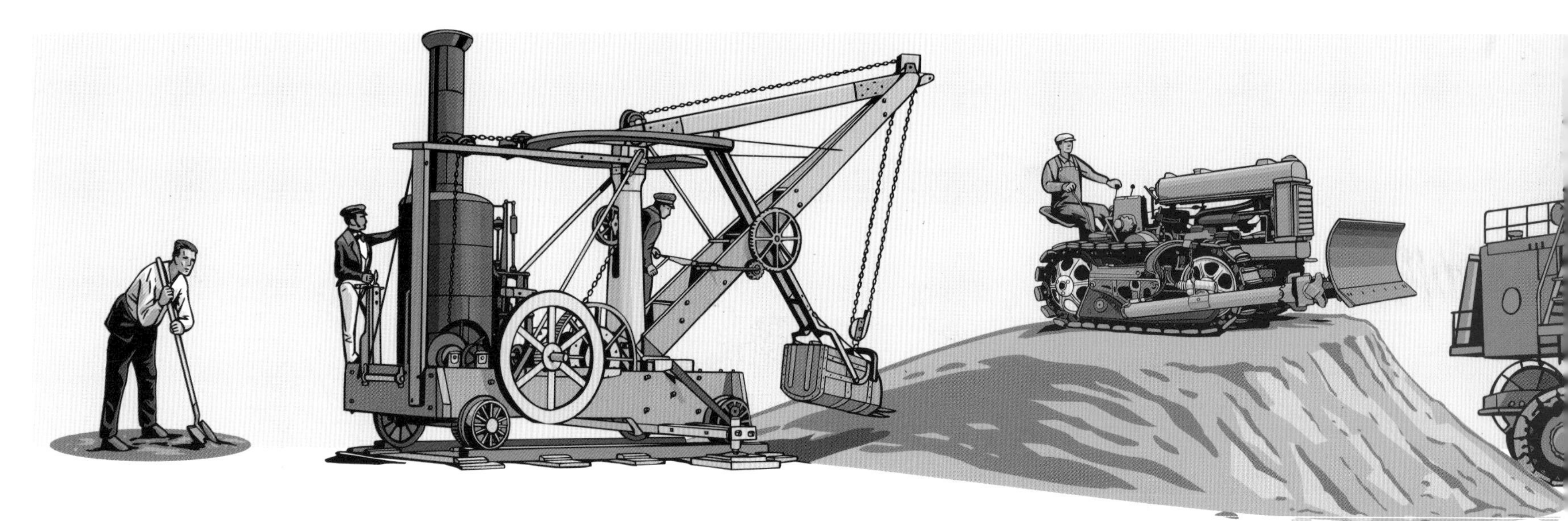

which giant machines are capable of doing extraordinary tasks that affect people's lives every day. Giant bulldozers clear the way for highways. Huge stripping shovels remove piles of coal the size of a small house high into the air. Enormous oil rigs drill far out at sea. Even if we do not see the machines at work, they make our lives easier every time we drive on a highway or turn on the lights at home.

Wow!

Giant machines are fascinating. The wonders of a construction site are captivating to everyone, from the casual observer to the expert builder. People like to build and shape an environment so that it becomes something else. So we build sand castles at the beach, create beautiful backyard gardens, shift mountains of earth, build skyscrapers, and dig tunnels. Heavy equipment helps us change our environment in a way that human muscle alone cannot. Big machines allow people to be bigger than themselves-and in the case of the machines described in this book, a lot bigger.

Road Construction

There are more than 3.9 million miles of road in the United States, enough to circle the globe 150 times. Every road construction project requires heavy equipment to clear the way, carve a path, and lay the covering materials that make the road. Highway construction is complicated, requiring whole fleets of heavy equipment, each responsible for a specific task. After the highway is built, even more equipment is needed to maintain and repair the roads.

An excavator is an all-purpose machine with special attachments that dig holes, lift roots out of the ground, and do a lot of other jobs. Because the excavator can do so many things, it is one of the most frequently used pieces of equipment at construction sites.

The bulldozer is usually among the first pieces of equipment needed on a highway construction project. The front blade, called a dozer, pushes aside trees, rocks, bushes, earth, and anything else that gets in the way. An attachment on the rear called a ripper is like a knife that can be jammed into the ground and dragged to loosen the compacted earth, rocks, and roots below.

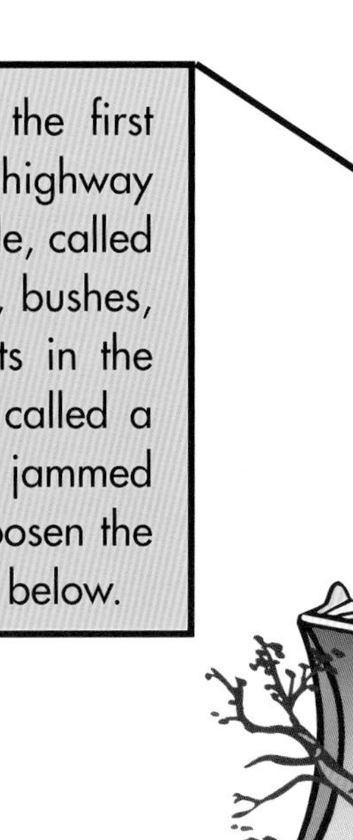

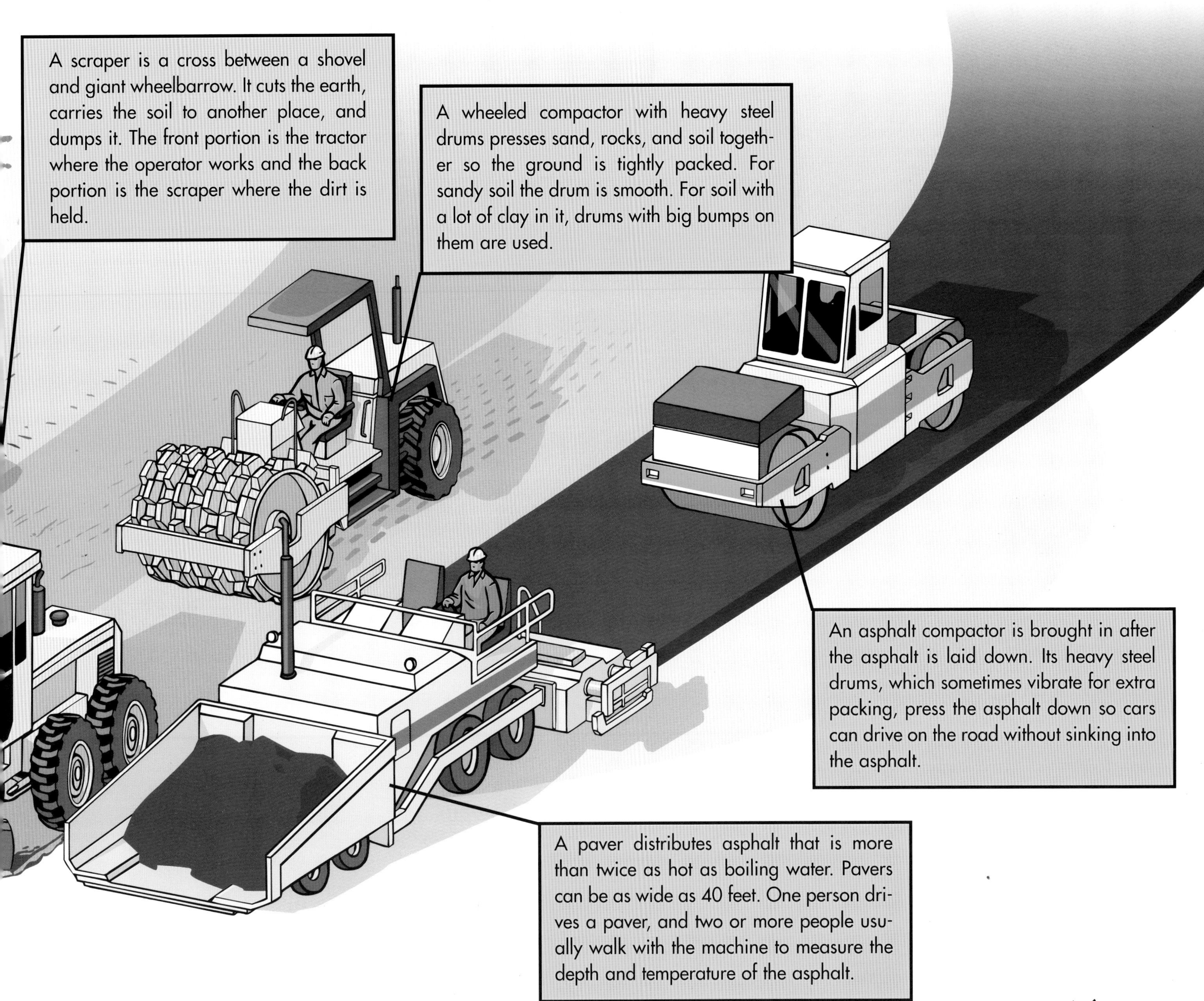
A scraper is a cross between a shovel and giant wheelbarrow. It cuts the earth, carries the soil to another place, and dumps it. The front portion is the tractor where the operator works and the back portion is the scraper where the dirt is held.
A wheeled compactor with heavy steel drums presses sand, rocks, and soil together so the ground is tightly packed. For sandy soil the drum is smooth. For soil with a lot of clay in it, drums with big bumps on them are used.
An asphalt compactor is brought in after the asphalt is laid down. Its heavy steel drums, which sometimes vibrate for extra packing, press the asphalt down so cars can drive on the road without sinking into the asphalt.
A paver distributes asphalt that is more than twice as hot as boiling water. Pavers can be as wide as 40 feet. One person drives a paver, and two or more people usually walk with the machine to measure the depth and temperature of the asphalt.

Bulldozers

Bulldozers are big, tough, heavy machines that push things—especially dirt—from one place to another. They travel very slowly—a ten-year-old child can walk faster than most bulldozers—but they are very strong. They knock down trees, push dirt around, and clear the way for the other machines at the construction site.

Bulldozers, which were called tractor crawlers when they were first invented, are used for many other purposes. Sometimes their metal blades are used to protect firefighters as they put out oil fires. Large pieces of metal at the back are called rippers, and are used to break up dirt and rip out tree stumps and rocks. Armies use bulldozers a great deal. As a matter of fact, the first tanks were made by modifying bulldozers.

The word bulldozer was around long before the first bulldozer machines. More than 100 years ago, the word "bulldoze" meant to bully a person and a bulldozer was the person doing the bullying. It wasn't until the 1920s that people started calling "tractor crawlers" bulldozers, or just "dozers."

The Double Dude Blade

The longest dozer blade ever made is 48 feet long—as long as five cars sitting in a row. It was so wide it needed two tractor crawlers to push it around. The blade was set at an angle to push dirt off to the side.

That's a Big Dozer!

The biggest bulldozer weighs 150 tons—that's heavier than 5,000 seven-year-old children. Its blade is 25 feet wide and 16 feet tall, which is the size of a highway billboard. It is usually used to push dirt at coal mines. It would take one person with a shovel an entire month to move as much dirt as this dozer pushes in ten minutes.

Underwater Bulldozer

In Asia, workers sometimes use an underwater, or amphibious, bulldozer to work in a harbor and river. The tall stack looks like a periscope but it is more like a radio tower. Nobody sits inside this bulldozer. Instead, an operator on land makes it move with a control box. Some amphibious bulldozers can work in water up to 23 feet deep. They can travel faster going backwards than forwards.

Dozer Blades

Bulldozers use different kinds of blades for different uses.

1. The most common blade is a straight blade. It has a relatively flat front with reinforced metal at the bottom for cutting into the ground.

2. An angled blade is placed on an angle to move dirt and other material to the side, like a snowplow. It is usually used for preparing the ground for a new road.

3. The U blade is curved like the letter "U" to prevent material from spilling off the sides of the blade. This is used to move large amounts of material, but it is not very good at cutting into the ground.

4. A push blade is used by the biggest bulldozers. It is made of heavier, stronger metal with extra metal plates to push big, heavy piles of dirt and rocks.

Scrapers

A scraper's job is to pick up dirt, move it, and then drop it into a new location. Using very powerful engines, most scrapers have a "bowl" in the back with a sharp cutting edge on the bottom. The cutter is dropped into the ground and the scraper is driven forward. The soil curls up into the bowl like butter on a knife. When the bowl is filled, the driver lifts the cutter and closes the "apron," which is like a door, to contain the dirt. The scraper then carries its load to a new location where the dirt is dumped. Scrapers are usually used to prepare the way for building a road, dam, or building site.

The most difficult part of a scraper's job is getting enough power to pull the cutter through the dirt. Often, bulldozers or other scrapers will help push the scraper while it is digging into the dirt. Scraper engines are even more powerful than bulldozers' and are at least ten times as strong as a family car. The largest scraper can hold more than 40 tons of soil, which is about the weight of eight elephants.

The driver of a double-engine scraper has a lot to think about. He not only has to steer the scraper, but also run two engines and operate the bowl, apron, and ejector.

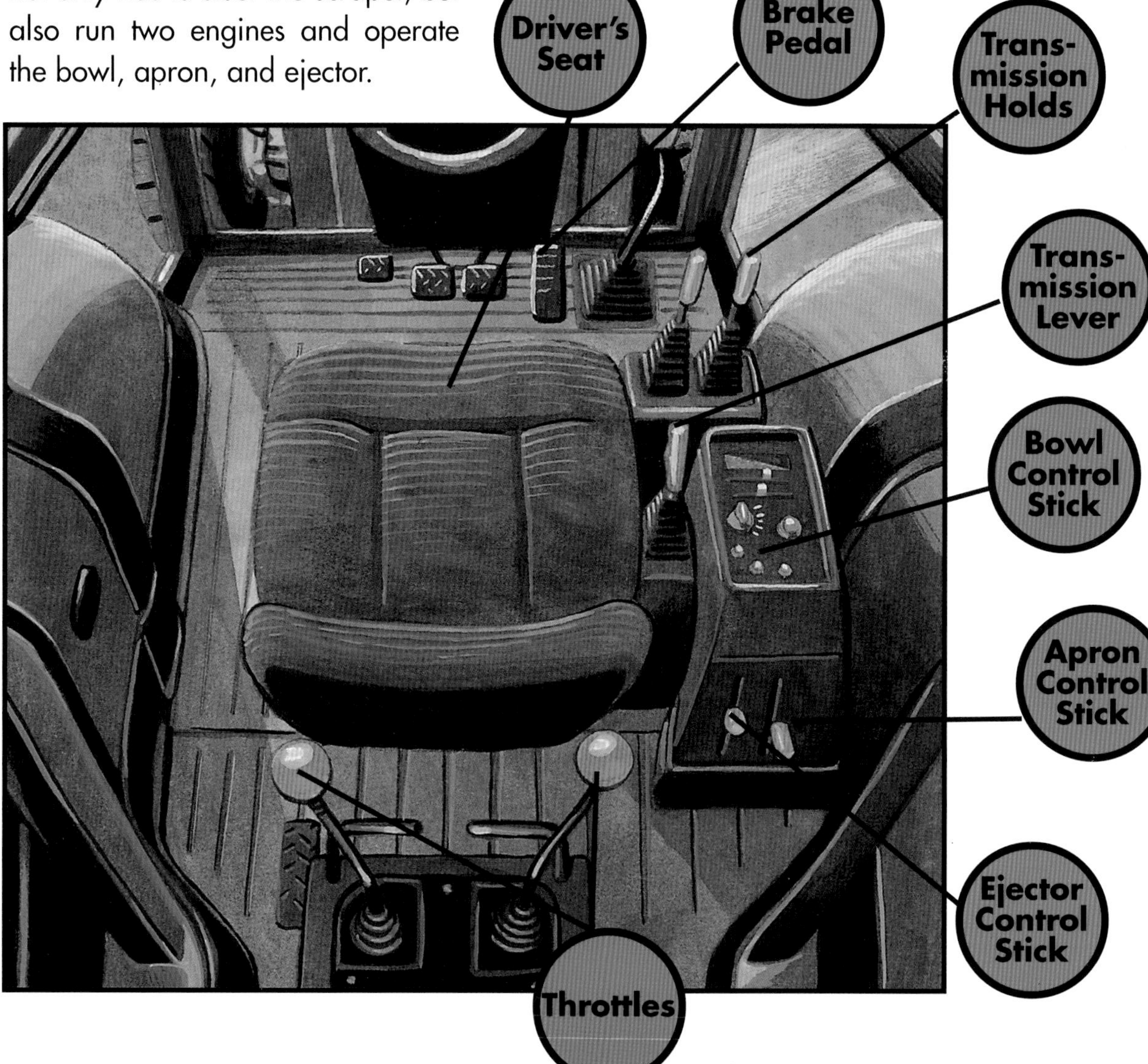

1. Single-Engine Scraper

There are three basic types of scrapers. The simplest is the single-engine tractor that pulls an open bowl. Usually, this kind of scraper is not strong enough to pick up soil without help from a bulldozer or another scraper. This is why scrapers have extra strong rear sections—other machines can push it from behind while the scraper is cutting the dirt.

2. Double-Engine Scraper

A double-engine scraper has an extra engine in the back to give it additional power. Even with two engines, though, a scraper sometimes needs extra help. Often two scrapers will work together, taking turns pushing or pulling each other as they scrape dirt into their bowls. This can be very complicated work and requires a lot of skill and teamwork.

3. Self-Loading Scraper

A self-loading, or elevating, scraper has a special "elevator" in the front of the bowl with lots of long metal scoops that cut into the dirt and then lift the dirt into the bowl like an escalator. Self-loading scrapers are not very good at digging rocks or hard soil and they cost more to run than other scrapers.

Robert LeTourneau was one of the most important inventors of heavy equipment. He dropped out of school when he was 14, but was able to teach himself how to design and build scrapers. One of his inventions was the 200-foot-long Electric Digger, which was longer than three tractor-trailer trucks. Run by eight engines, it was the biggest scraper ever made. The company LeTourneau created grew to become one of the most important manufacturers of heavy equipment in the United States. LeTourneau gave away most of the money he made, primarily to schools. Even though he did not get a proper education when he was young, he thought it was very important that everyone go to school and get a good education.

Loaders

Front-end loaders are very useful machines, serving many different purposes. Armed with a wide bucket in front, they can pick up materials, carry them, and dump them. Some loaders have tracks like bulldozers, but most use wheels, which allow them to drive on roads. Loaders are frequently used on construction sites, in gravel pits and mines, and at docks. Special attachments are often added for loading logs onto trucks in forestry work. Many smaller loaders have small excavators attached to the rear called backhoes, which are used for digging.

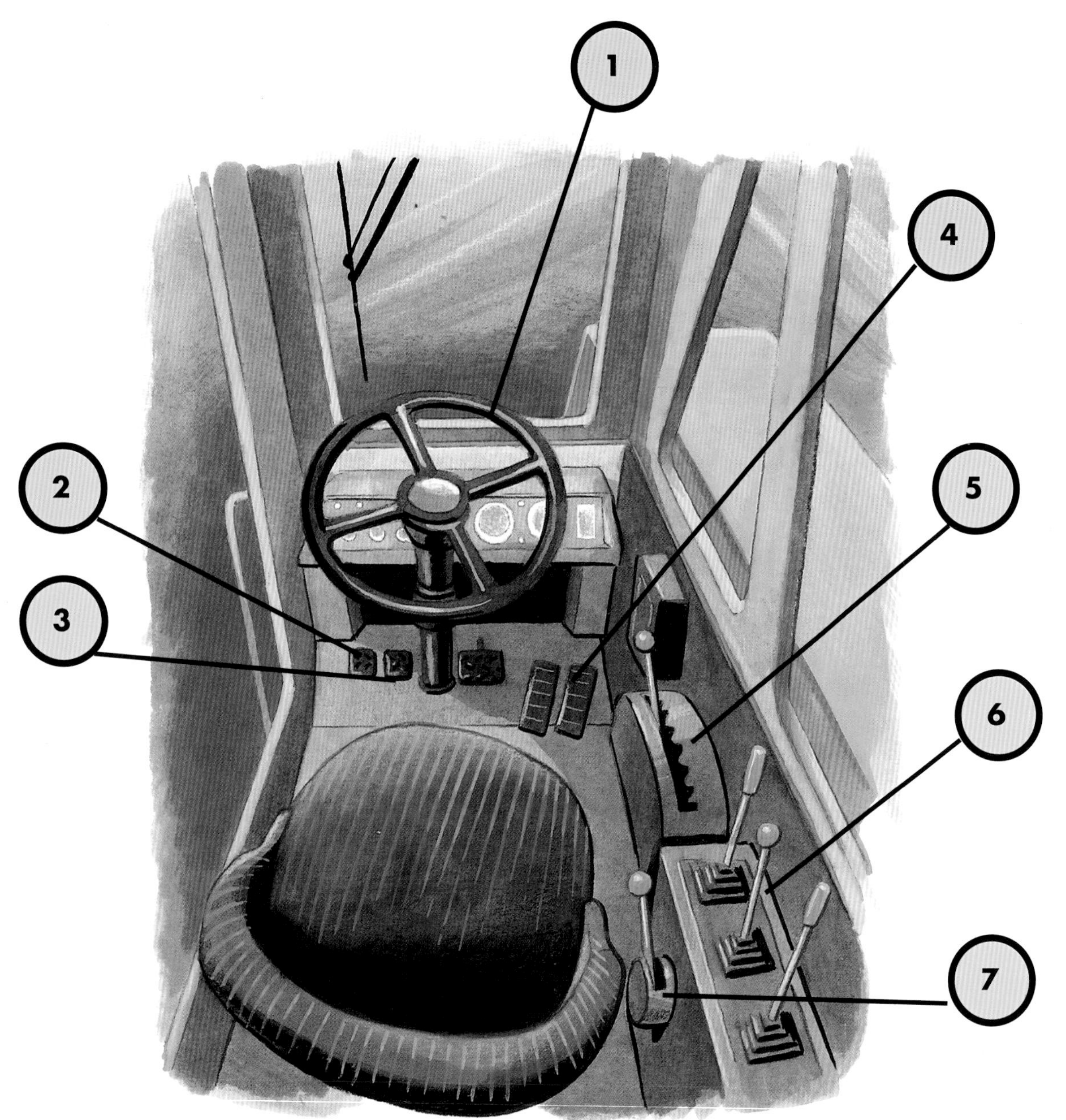

Multiple Controls

A loader with a backhoe attachment has three sets of controls, one to drive the machine and the other two to operate the front loader and backhoe.

1. **Steering wheel and driving controls**
2. **Dump pedal**
3. **Brake pedals**
4. **Accelerator**
5. **Loader control levers**
6. **Backhoe control levers**
7. **Stabilizer jack controls**

Mechanized Dancer

Loader operators constantly have to move their machines back and forth and lift the bucket up and down. Operators will often make 500 moves in an hour. Some loaders bend in the middle to help them make turns in tight spaces.

The largest loaders are used in mines to lift large rocks and huge hunks of dirt, coal, and other materials. This giant loader can lift 100,000 pounds, or enough sand to build 30,000 sand castles at the beach. It is 20 feet tall and 58 feet long, making it the same size as a tractor-trailer truck. Its arm can reach 39 feet, or as high as a four-story building. The bucket is 21 feet wide, which means a large van could fit in it with room to spare.

Paving Machines

Roads are made by placing layers of different materials on top of each other. The top layer is usually made of asphalt or concrete placed on the road by paving machines. Asphalt pavers are big, awkward-looking machines that are very hot, smelly, and noisy. Hot tar combined with sand, gravel, and crushed stones are placed in the hopper (a big box with a hole). As the asphalt mixture falls through the hole, conveyors carry it to the back of the machine. An auger, which is like a giant corkscrew, spreads the asphalt as it falls off the conveyor and onto the ground. A very heavy attachment called a screed then presses the mixture down. Finally, a soleplate goes over the asphalt to flatten and smooth it, similar to the way an iron flattens clothes.

1. Dump truck places hot asphalt into a giant paver

2. Hopper contains the asphalt mixture

3. Conveyor belt carries the asphalt to the rear of the paver

4. Auger slowly spreads the asphalt across the width of the machine.

5. Screed presses the asphalt into the ground

6. Soleplate flattens the asphalt

7. Workers measure the asphalt's height and temperature

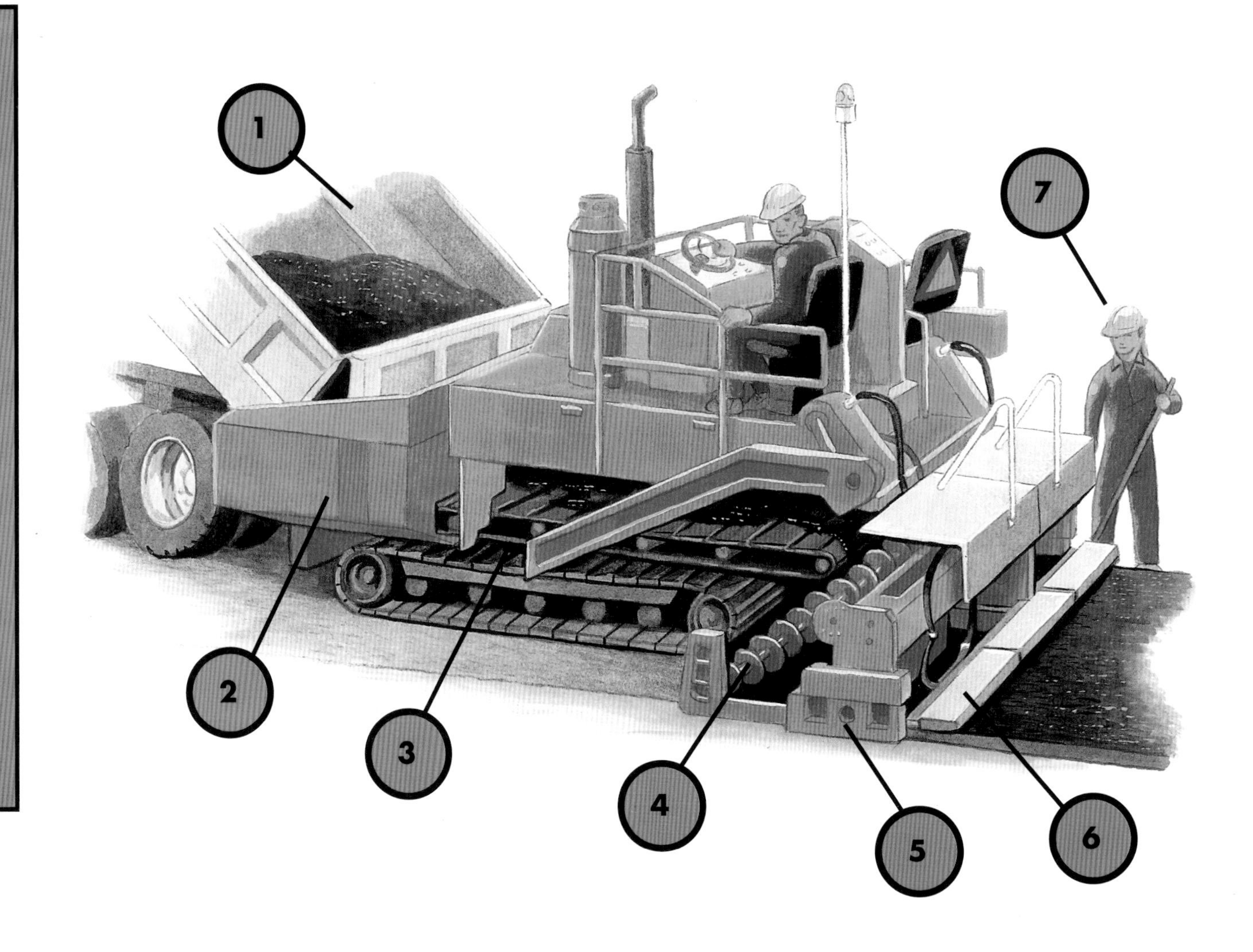

Asphalt Talk

Asphalt, the top layer of most roads, is made from crushed stone, sand, limestone, and bitumen (a black tar created when refining oil). The asphalt provides a hard, waterproof surface. It is usually used as the top layer of a road, with at least two other layers of gravel, sand, cement, and other materials beneath it. Although asphalt is almost always made in special plants, there are places in the world where it can be found in nature.

Concrete Paver

Concrete pavers are like asphalt pavers but without the heat. As a truck unloads wet concrete into the machine, the auger (the giant corkscrew) spreads it across the width of the pavement. A screed flattens the concrete and removes extra material. Some new concrete pavers can place steel rods into the wet concrete, making the roadway stronger.

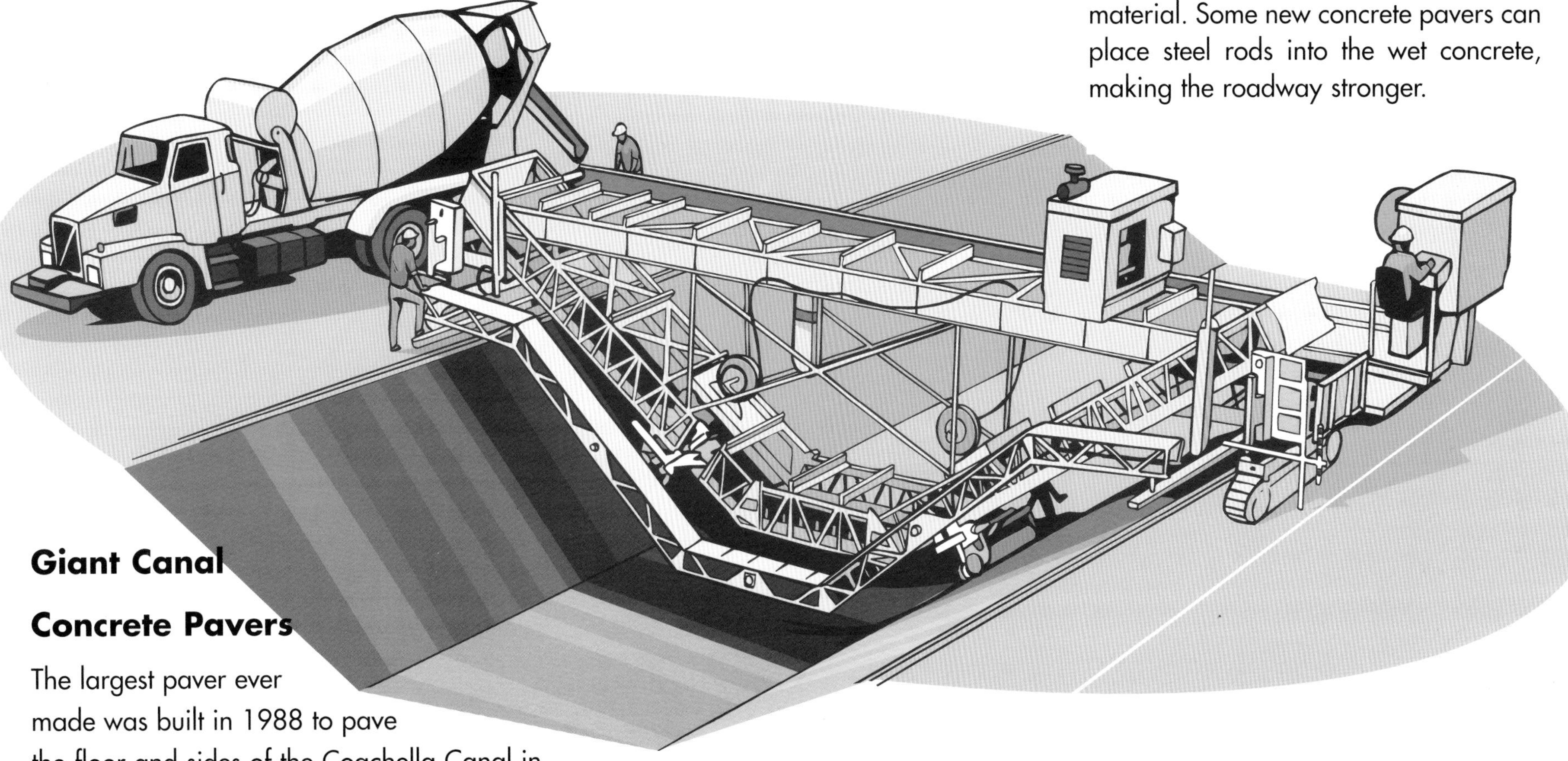

Giant Canal Concrete Pavers

The largest paver ever made was built in 1988 to pave the floor and sides of the Coachella Canal in California. The machine was shaped like an upside down triangle, 103 feet wide at the top and 48 feet wide at the bottom to pave the canal's steep slopes.

Excavators

Excavator means digger, but these very useful machines do many more things than dig. Using special attachments, a hydraulic excavator can tear down a building, dig a trench, load a truck, dig up an underground tank, pulverize a concrete wall into dust, and many other tasks. When you drive by a construction site on the road you are very likely to see an excavator. One out of every three pieces of heavy equipment sold is a hydraulic excavator.

Excavators are almost never used for carrying things very far. Usually, they are on slow-moving crawlers that travel at about the same speed as a ten-year-old walking. This is because even though an excavator has a large engine, most of its power is devoted to operating its large hydraulic arm. Excavators with wheels can move around more and drive on roads, but they are usually not very big or powerful.

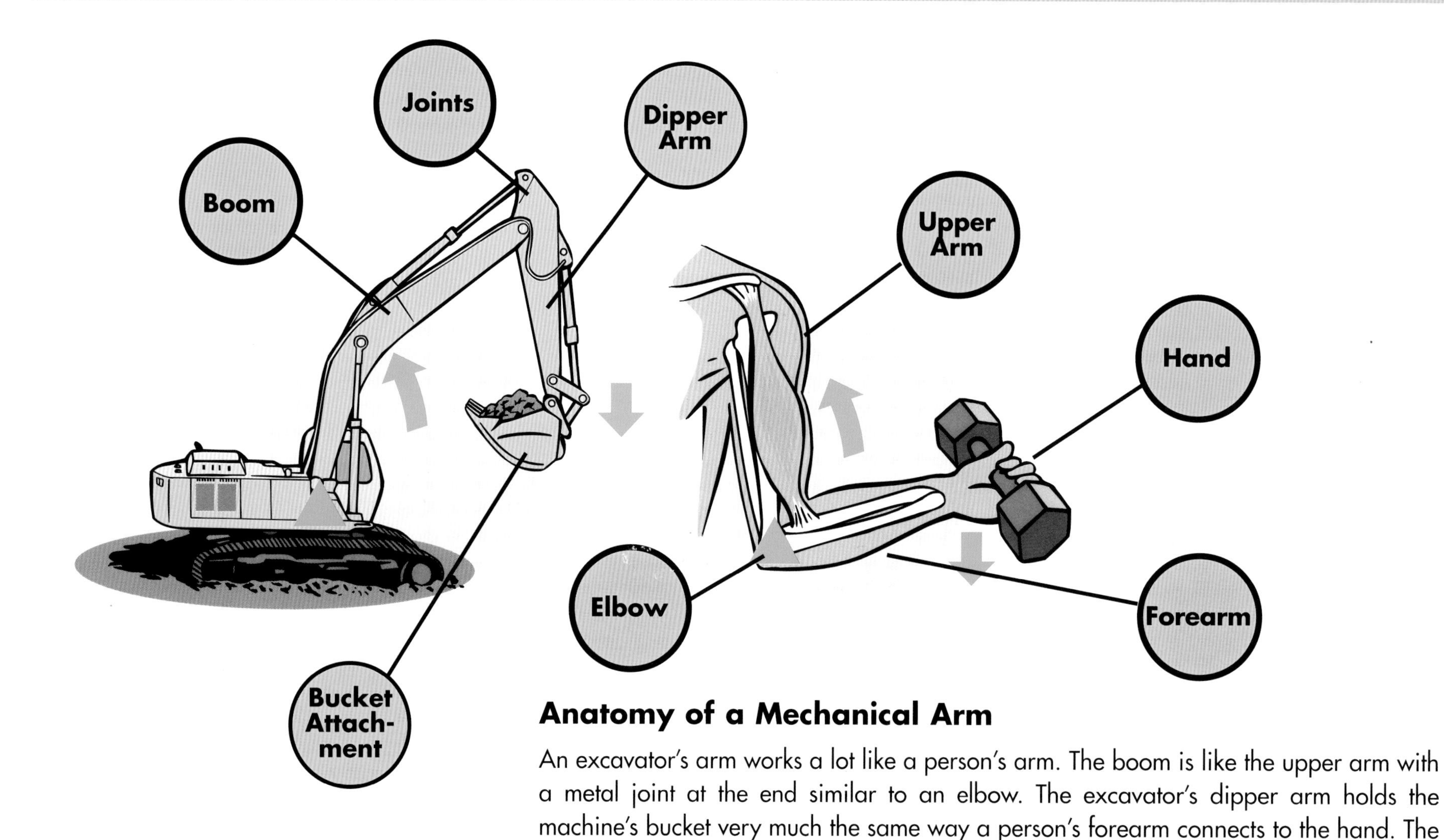

Anatomy of a Mechanical Arm

An excavator's arm works a lot like a person's arm. The boom is like the upper arm with a metal joint at the end similar to an elbow. The excavator's dipper arm holds the machine's bucket very much the same way a person's forearm connects to the hand. The hydraulic rams act like muscles maneuvering the arm up, down, and around.

Long Reach

One of the great advantages of using a hydraulic excavator for digging is the machine's long reach. The excavator's reach is almost as deep into the ground as it is high into the air. The arm can also swing around to the side for digging and dumping.

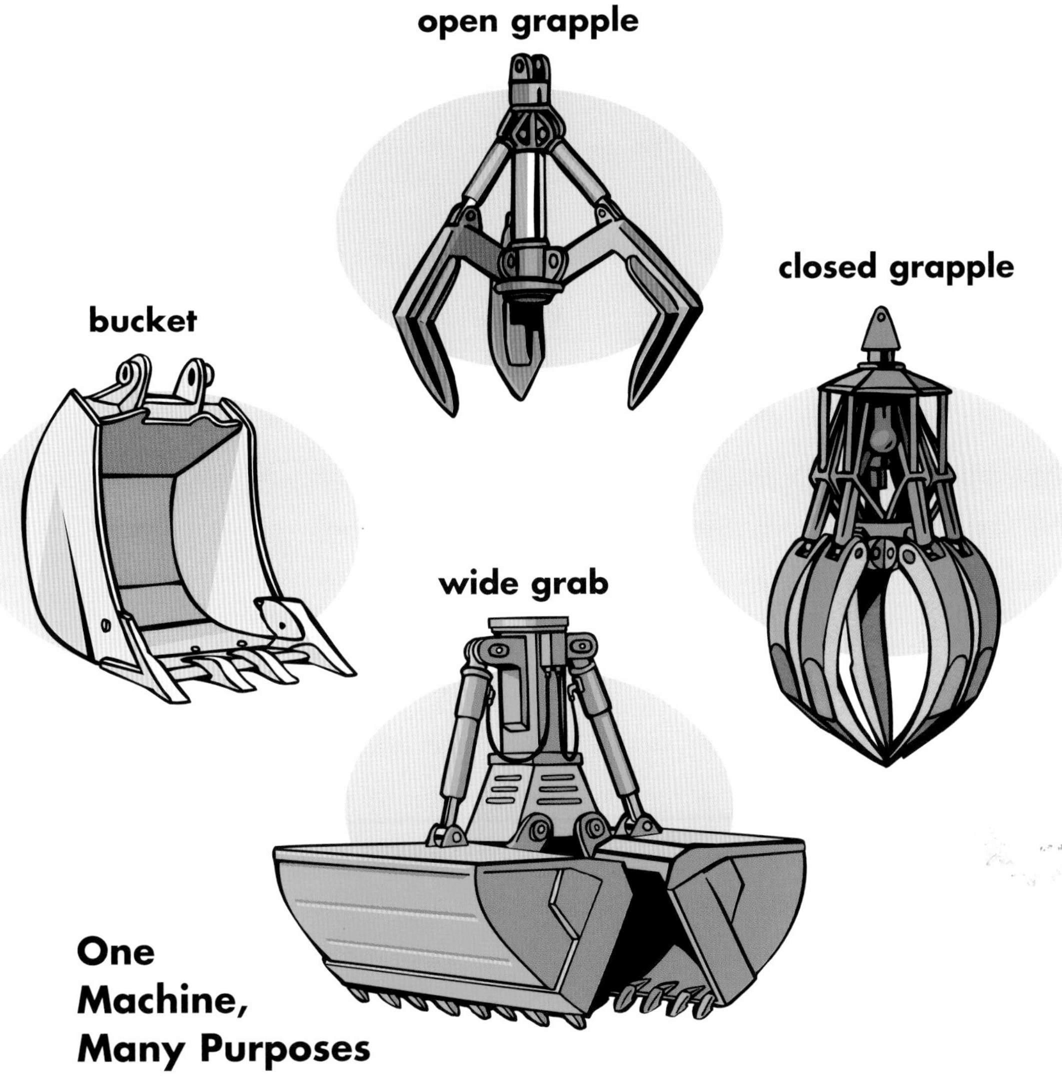

One Machine, Many Purposes

A steel bucket that digs inward is the most common item found at the end of an excavator's arm, but there are many other types of attachments. These include grabbers, stump cutters, compactors, trenchers, asphalt cutters, and jackhammers.

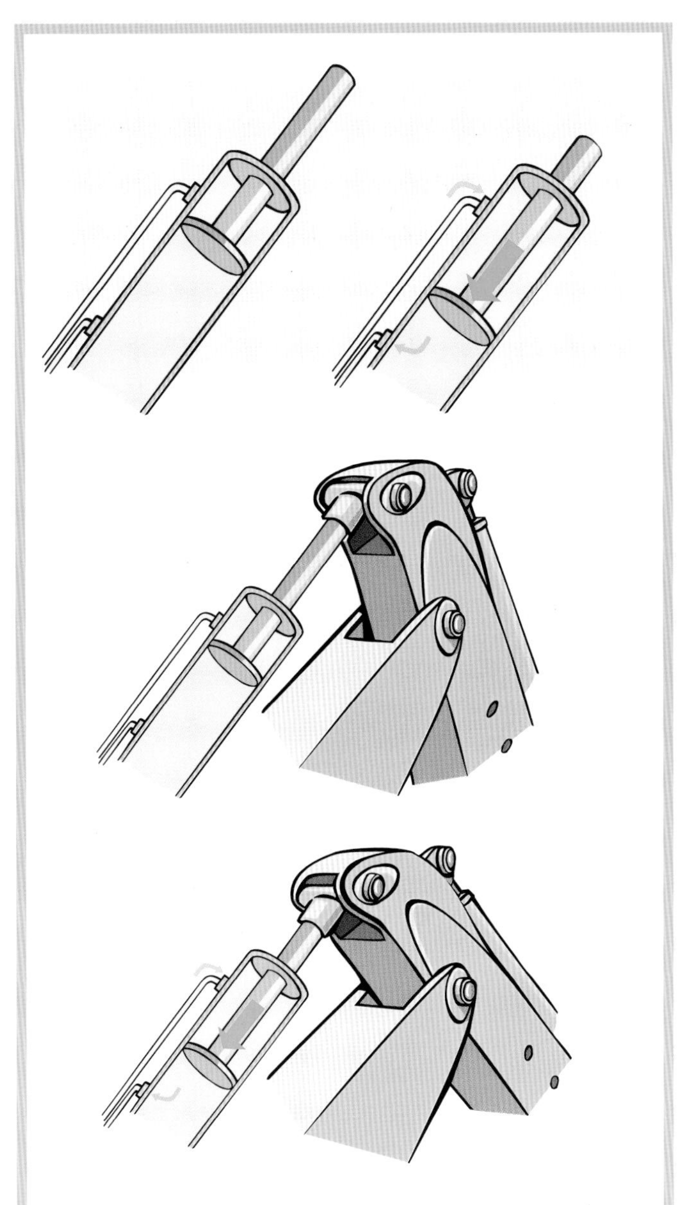

Many powerful machines use hydraulic systems. Hydraulics are based on the fact that liquids cannot be squeezed. When you push a liquid, it pushes out somewhere else. Hydraulic fluid is a thin oil that is used to push different parts of a machine. The engine forces the fluid into cylinders that then push pistons outward. The pistons are designed to do different jobs. In an excavator, hydraulic pistons powered by the central engine move the excavator's arm and its attachment.

Trenchers

Looking like giant chain saws, trenchers dig ditches. The biggest trenchers weigh as much as 15 elephants. They make the earth shake as they carve four-foot-wide holes as deep as 20 feet into the ground. That is twice as deep as the deep end of most swimming pools. Armed with a gigantic boom, a giant chain with extra-strong metal blades cuts through rocks, frozen earth, and almost anything else that gets in the way.

Giant trenchers are perfect for digging long ditches for underground cables, wires, and pipes. The advantage of using a trencher over other digging machines is that it removes as little material as possible, so the ditch does not have to be any wider than the pipe or cable that will lie at the bottom. As the boom carries the earth into the machine, the dirt falls onto a second conveyor that takes it off to the side. This makes it relatively simple to push the dirt back into the ditch after the pipe or cable is in place.

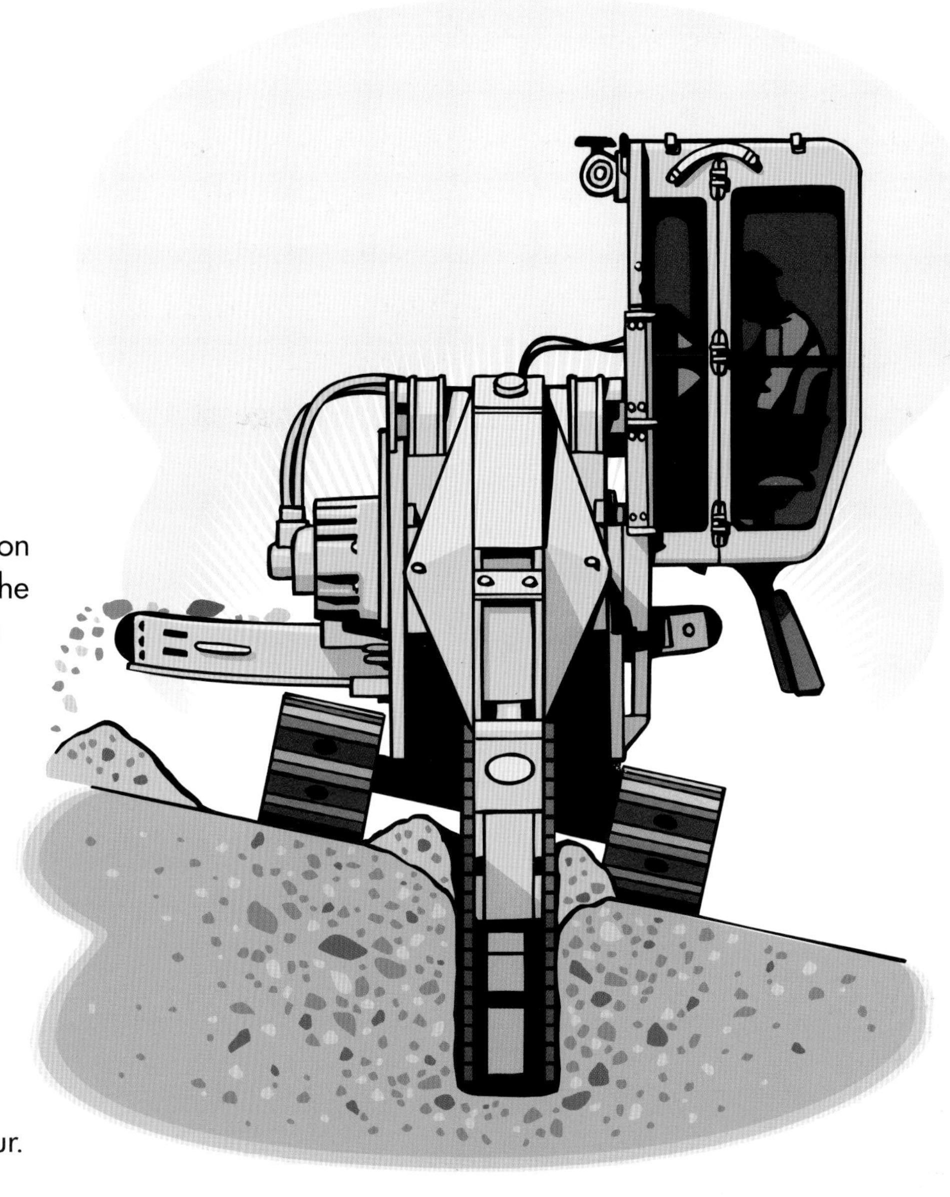

Steady as She Goes

The first trencher consisted of a series of buckets on a belt that went around and around. Some of the earliest heavy equipment, made hundreds of years ago, were designed like this. Today's trenchers, however, are much more powerful.

Some trenchers are designed so that the machine can tilt into a hillside, and cut a perfectly vertical ditch straight down into the ground. Special features also allow the machine to automatically dig a ditch with a flat bottom in spite of bumps in the ground. Depending on ground conditions, a typical trencher with a ten-foot boom can dig a 50-foot long trench that is four feet deep in about an hour.

Backyard Trenchers

Trenchers come in all sizes. Some are small enough to be operated by hand, with two- or three-foot booms. Nevertheless, they are difficult to operate, weighing hundreds of pounds. Many trenchers have attachments that allow the machine to place a cable in the ditch as it is being excavated and then push the dirt back into the ditch.

Rock Cutter

In some cases where the rock is too hard for a trencher, a rock-cutter attachment is used. Made with stronger metal and narrower than a trencher, a rock cutter can cut solid rock. It is basically a very big, very strong power saw. The alternative to a rock cutter for cutting stone is usually explosives, such as dynamite.

Mobile Cranes

Mobile cranes are like weightlifters on wheels. As big as tractor-trailer trucks, the biggest crane can pick up a load heavier than a house, lift it hundreds of feet into the air, and place it on top of a 40-story building. And when it is done, it can just drive away to the next job.

How can it do this? Through strong equipment and powerful engines, and through the use of levers and pulleys. If a person is not strong enough to lift a heavy object he or she can use a rope and a pulley to lift it and place it in a new spot. A crane works in the same way, except it uses big metal booms, steel cables, and powerful engines.

There are many different kinds of mobile cranes. Some are on wheels and some are on crawlers. Some drive on roads, others have to be carried on the back of trucks. The biggest mobile cranes can lift a million pounds or more. Even the smallest ones can lift 10,000 pounds, the same weight as an elephant. A special kind of mobile crane you often see on the road is a loader crane, which is a small crane mounted on the back of truck bed to lift materials on and off the truck. But all mobile cranes use the same principles of levers and pulleys and they all do the same basic job.

This Liebherr LTM 1400 mobile crane can lift objects as heavy as 100,000 pounds (or eight school buses filled with children) to the top of a 40-story building.

Spectacular Attachments

Using extra attachments, a mobile crane can lift even heavier objects from far away. But as you can see, it can get pretty complicated. The simplest way to lift something is to just use the main boom. The derrick gives the crane extra strength to pick up heavier objects. To give the crane better stability so it doesn't tip over, workers sometimes add extra counterweights or suspended ballast at the back.

A luffing jib can be added to the top of the crane to give it a longer reach. When this is done, though, the workers must be very careful not to pick up something too heavy because the crane is more likely to tip over. Just like when a person lifts a heavy weight, it's easier to lift something straight up than to reach out and pick it up.

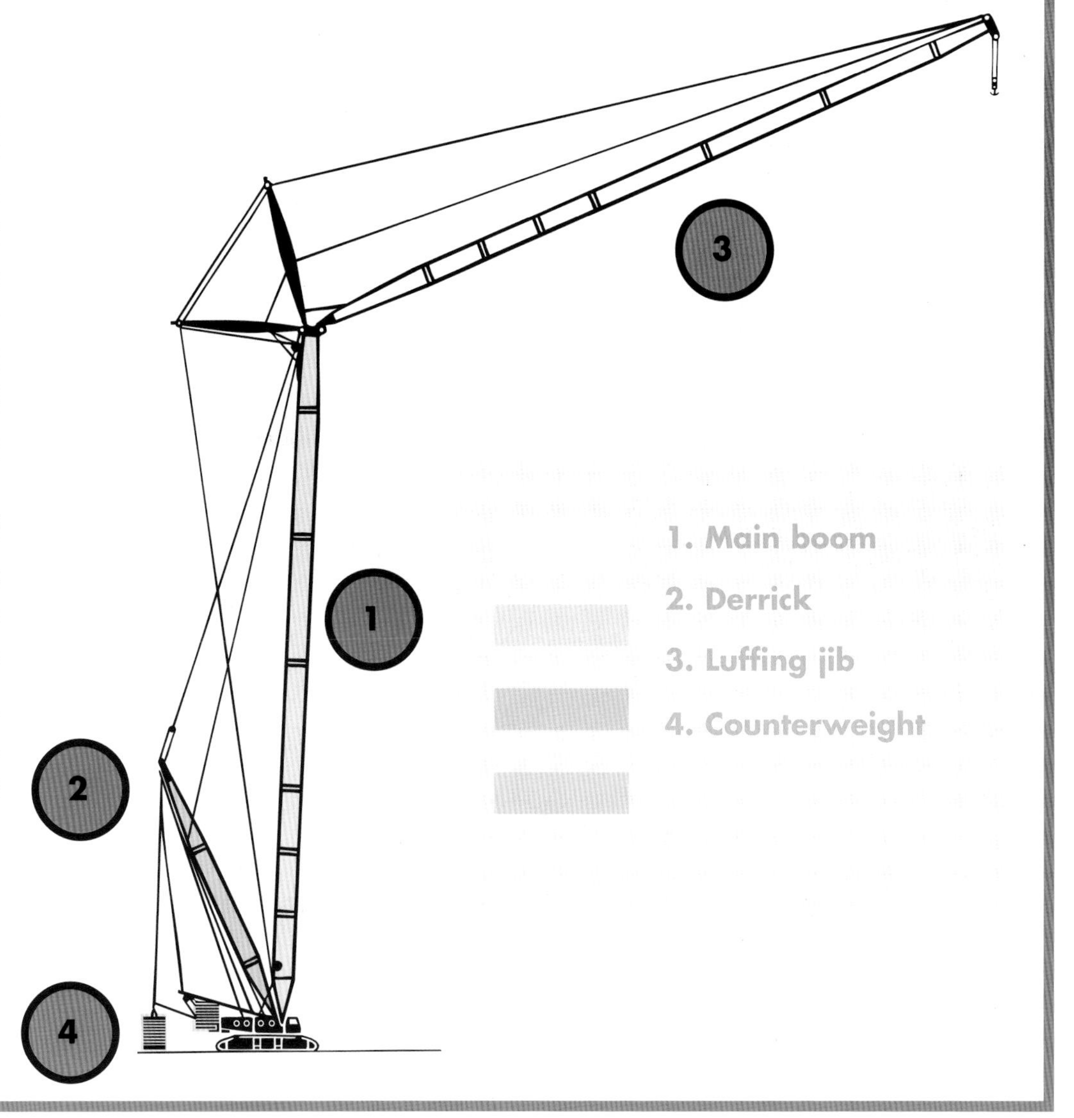

Reach For It

All wheeled cranes have outriggers to make the crane more stable and prevent the crane from tipping over. These special jacks reach out from the main truck to spread the weight of the crane and widen its base.

Tower Cranes

Imagine two Statues of Liberty standing on top of each other and the top one has a metal arm reaching out as long as a football field. That's how big the biggest tower cranes are. They are so big that when they are built, a smaller crane is needed at the top to build the upper portions of the main crane. The hook weighs more than a minivan. Pieces for a giant tower crane can sometimes fill up to 100 trucks. Putting them all together can cost as much as one million dollars. But when the work is done, the crane is a super-powerful lifter, capable of lifting objects weighing hundreds of thousands of pounds.

Tower cranes are the tallest cranes in the world. They are used to help build skyscrapers, giant power plants, and off-shore drilling platforms. They are stronger than mobile cranes and can reach farther. The main problem with a tower crane is that if you want to move it, you usually have to dismantle the whole machine, move the pieces individually, and then put it back together again.

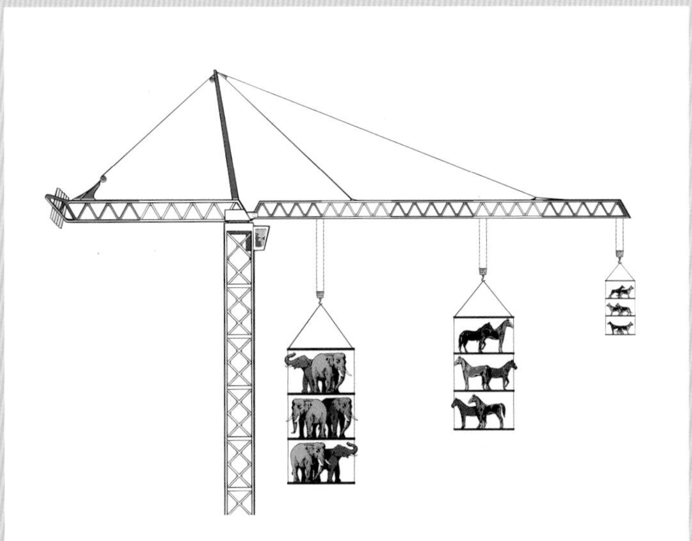

Anyone who climbs trees knows that the farther out on a limb you go, the more likely it is the branch will break. Cranes work the same way. The closer a load is to the mast of a tower crane or the main boom of a mobile crane, the more the crane can lift. Similarly, the farther out on the jib the load is, the lighter it has to be to prevent it from tipping the crane over.

"Give Me a Place to Stand"

Thousands of years ago builders used ancient cranes, called swapes, to lift and move objects that were too heavy for their arms and backs. Although these ancient cranes were made of wood and rope, they used the same principles as today's giant cranes. A swape had a lever secured to a fixed position from which it did its heavy lifting. A heavy weight was added to the opposite end of the boom to provide extra weight and stability.

Archimedes, a Greek scientist from long ago, was one of the great engineers of the ancient world. "Give me a place to stand on and I will move the earth," he once said. He designed several cranes, including one called a ship-shaking machine for defending a fort from ships. The giant crane had a claw at the end of it which swung out over the walls of a fort and grabbed onto the bottom of an attacking ship. Using levers and pulleys, men inside the fort then pulled the claw up, taking the ship with it.

"A ship was frequently lifted to a great height in the air—a dreadful thing to behold—and was rolled to and fro, and kept swinging, until the mariners were all thrown out, when at length it was dashed against the rocks, or was dropped," the Greek historian Plutarch wrote.

Tower Cranes vs. Mobile Cranes

When a crane is needed for a construction job, someone must decided what kind of crane to use. They have to choose between a mobile crane and a tower crane. Each one has advantages and disadvantages. The advantage of a tower crane is that it uses less surface area on the ground, is stronger and more stable, reaches higher and farther into the sky, has faster lifting speeds, and can better withstand high winds.

The advantage of a mobile crane is that it is much easier to move from site to site and is less expensive. If more lifting capacity is needed, it has special attachments that can make it almost as strong as a tower crane.

Generally speaking, tower cranes are used for very big building projects that do not have a lot of space for equipment to move around. Builders will often use both kinds of cranes, especially for tall structures. While mobile cranes lift and move materials at the base of the structure, a large tower crane built on top of a building can maneuver objects from high above.

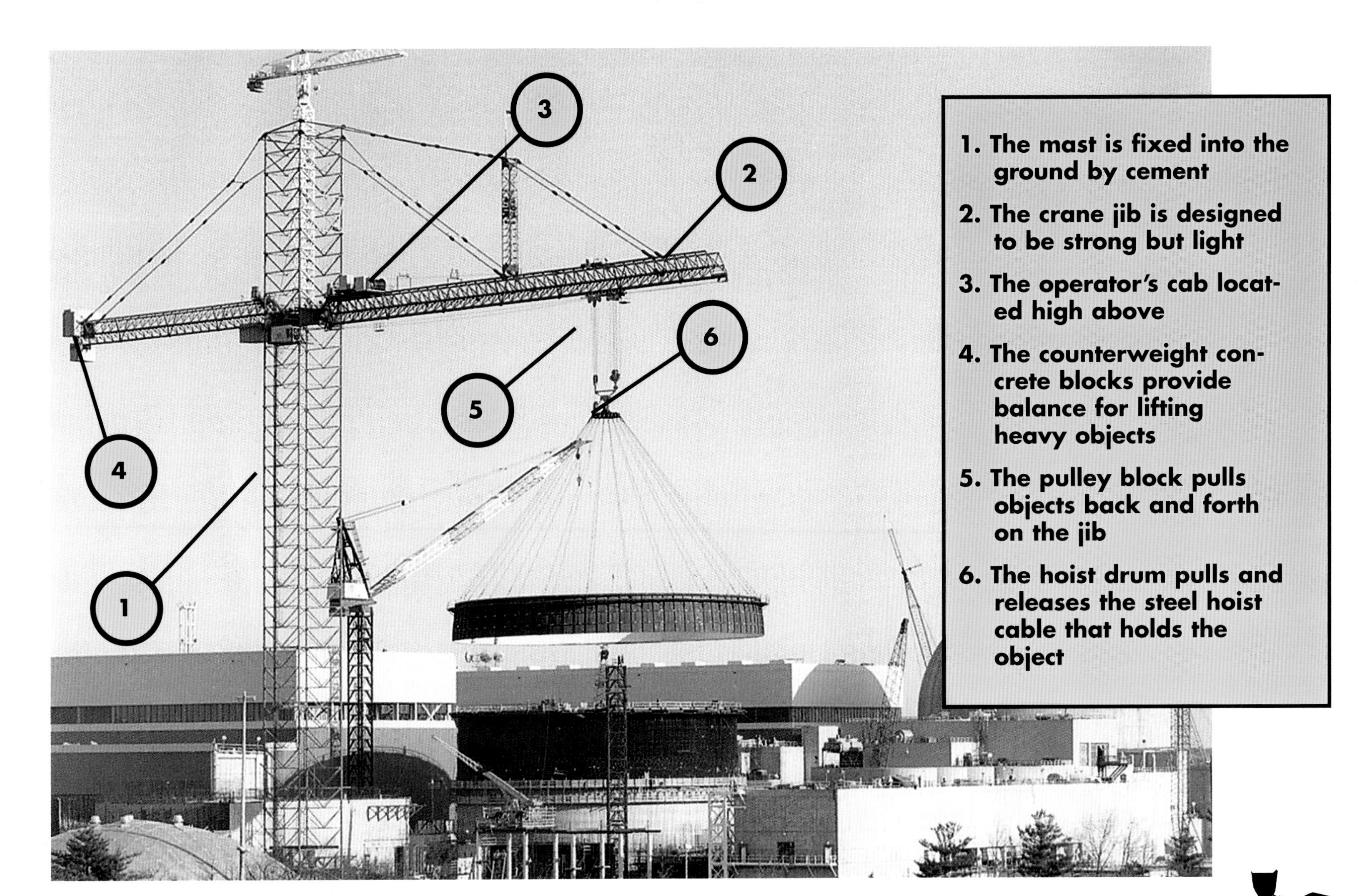

Giant Hydraulic Excavators

Unlike their smaller cousins which can do many different jobs, giant hydraulic excavators essentially serve one purpose—digging, and usually in strip mines. With a bucket the size of a bulldozer, a giant hydraulic excavator can scoop heaps of rocks and dirt weighing as much as 100,000 pounds. That is as heavy as the full lineups of eight professional football teams. It usually takes about 25 seconds to complete a load-lift-dump-and-return cycle.

The dimensions of the largest excavators are enormous: 60 feet long, 35 feet tall, and 18 feet wide. They are as big as a large three-story building. The fuel tanks can hold up to 2,500 gallons, or the same as 50 bathtubs filled with gasoline. The machines weigh more than one million pounds and run on engines as powerful as 3,500 horses.

The first mechanically operated excavating machine was the Otis Steam Excavator. It was invented in the 1830s by William Otis Smith to help build a railroad in Massachusetts. The machine was pulled on railroad tracks by a team of horses. It used steam power to lift a bucket and swung with a boom handled by two men.

Tiny compared to today's machines, the Otis Steam Excavator made it much easier for men who would otherwise use shovels and brute strength for digging. A newspaper at the time hailed it as "a great saving of labor" that did "the work of 50 men."

What a Load!

The most common use of a hydraulic excavator for mining purposes is for loading giant trucks. The truck backs in on the left side of the machine for loading. The left side is preferred because then the excavator operator directly faces the truck driver. It usually takes three or four bucket loads to fill the back of a truck, taking about two minutes to complete.

Stripping Shovels

Giant hydraulic excavators do the job that electric mining shovels have done for many years. The bigger strip mining shovels can hold even more rock and dirt than massive hydraulic excavators. A giant mining shovel uses as much electricity in one month as 300 houses.

The world's biggest piece of heavy equipment was an electric shovel called The Captain. It weighed 28 million pounds (equal to the weight of more than 2,000 adult elephants), was as tall as 22-story building, and needed 36 giant engines to operate. Its crawlers were so big, you could drive a truck underneath with room to spare. Fire in the hydraulic system destroyed The Captain in 1991.

1. Hydraulic ram to raise and lower the operator arm

2. Sharp metal teeth for digging

3. Bucket empties a load

4. Platform swivels on a swing gear inside

5. Crawlers

Draglines

Draglines are the largest earth-moving machines in the world that use a single bucket for digging. In many ways they are very simple machines. Place a giant bucket at the end of two chains, hang the chains from a huge boom that looks like a crane, drop the bucket into a pit, and then drag it back up, scraping up mounds of dirt. That is basically what draglines do. The only thing is they are gigantic.

In mining, draglines are very good at removing what is called overburden. Overburden is the dirt the covers the coal, copper, gold, or other minerals that are buried deep under the ground. Draglines usually work from on top of the mine, removing huge heaps of dirt (three or four times as much as the biggest hydraulic excavator) as deep as 200 feet. The bucket lifts the dirt up out of the pit, swings to the side and then dumps the load. After the minerals have been remove, the dragline puts the "overburden" back into the mine.

Mining companies like to use draglines to remove overburden because they cost less money than stripping shovels and a fleet of mining trucks to use. Most of the places where there is coal and other minerals near the top of the ground have already been mined. That means companies have to dig deeper and deeper. Often, draglines are the cheapest machines to do the work for very large mining pits, even though it can cost as much as $40 million to build a giant one.

Giant Gulps

Draglines use giant steel buckets the size of three-car garages. One scoop of a giant bucket can dig, move, and dump more than 200 tons of dirt (enough to build 12,000 sand castles) to a new spot 100 yards away in less than 90 seconds. Working with a wheelbarrow for 12 hours a day, it would take one adult more than a month to accomplish the same job.

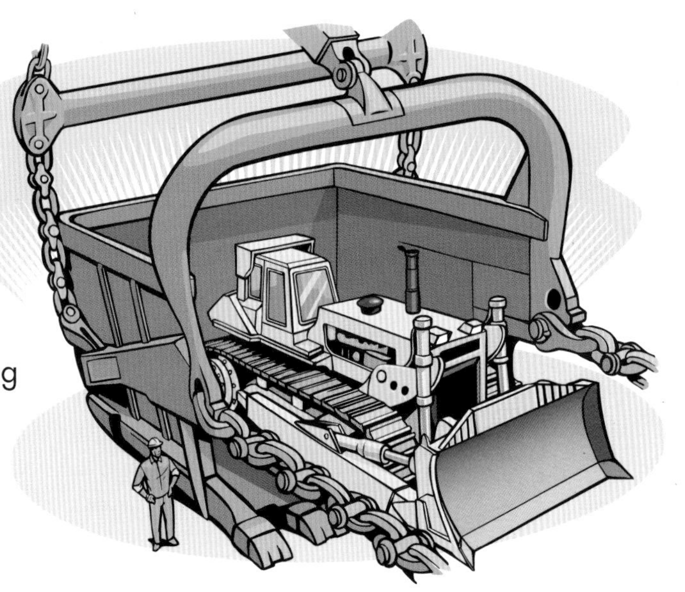

Too big for the biggest tires in the world, draglines use a special "walking" machine for moving. The system has giant "feet" on either side of the machine that are divided into two sections. Similar to a person walking, one of the sections is lifted and moved forward or backward, while the other sections hold up the machine. Once this action is completed, the other section does the same thing.

One Life, One Mine

Giant draglines are so big that companies usually buy them for just one mine. These are called "life-of-mine assets"—meaning they are supposed to last as long as the mine lasts. It usually takes three years just to design and build a dragline like this. Once built, they run day and night for as long as 30 or 40 years.

Big Muskie

The second biggest earthmover ever built was Big Muskie, a 27-million-pound machine that swung the largest bucket in history. It took three years to build Big Muskie at a coal mine near Zanesville, Ohio. More than 300 rail cars and 250 trucks carried the parts to build the machine.

When it was completed, Big Muskie was as tall as a 22-story building, as wide as an eight-lane highway, and almost one-tenth of a mile long. The bucket was 14 feet high, 27 feet wide, and 23 feet deep; meaning you could park six minivans in it. Its engines were as powerful as 1,000 large bulldozers. Big Muskie worked for 22 years before being shut down in 1991. It removed 608 million cubic yards of dirt, enough to fill more than a trillion backyard sandboxes.

1. **300-foot-long boom**
2. **Cab for two operators**
3. **Giant bucket**
4. **Walking pontoons**
5. **Machinery house holding as many as 40 motors**

Giant Mining Trucks

Huge. Gigantic. Monstrous. Titanic. Colossal. Immense. Mammoth. Pick a word that means big and that is what giant mining trucks are—only bigger. These trucks are so big they can't go on roads. If you visit a large mine, you will probably get to see one. Imagine, though, the biggest tractor-trailer truck you've ever seen on the road. Then imagine a truck that is twice as high and twice as wide. That is how big the biggest giant mining trucks are. They are four times bigger than the biggest truck you've ever seen.

The view from the driver's seat of a giant dump truck is a lot like an ordinary truck-except that it is 20 feet above the ground. Drivers take special courses to learn how to drive giant mining trucks. Some trucks now don't even use drivers. They run on computers.

Big Wheels

Giant mining trucks use six huge tires, each higher than a basketball hoop. Made of extra-strong material, they can cost up to $70,000 apiece. Tires for giant trucks don't just that have to be bigger than regular tires. They also have to be stronger. The heavier the truck and the faster it goes, the tougher the tire has to be. This is one of the reasons giant trucks do not go faster than 35 miles per hour.

1. V-shaped dump-truck floor helps to center the load
2. Ladder allows driver to climb to the driver's seat
3. Driver's cab is perched almost 20 feet above the ground
4. Canopy covers the driver's cab and engine from rocks
5. Each tire is twice as tall as a large, full-grown man

The largest dump truck in the world is the Caterpillar 797. It can carry as much as 360 tons—that's the same weight as 65 elephants. It is almost as high as a three-story building. When a Caterpillar 797 tips its load, it is taller than a five-story building.

Big Loads

Giant mining trucks do a very simple job. They carry dirt, coal, rocks, ore, and other materials from one place to another. One of their most common tasks is to carry dirt (called overburden) that covers the coal, ore, or mineral in a mine to another location. Then, that when the mining work is done, it refills the giant hole.

Lever's Away!

Dump trucks use levers to unload their rock piles. Whether the lever is a piece of wood, in a wheelbarrow, or in a 300-ton truck, the principle is the same. Levers turn on a fixed point called a fulcrum. The closer the pile of dirt is to the fulcrum, the less effort it takes to lift it and dump it onto the ground. You can try it yourself with a wheelbarrow or a piece of wood at home.

Bucket-Wheel Excavators

Imagine a large, steel-studded roller coaster at the end of an enormous steel bridge sticking out from a 15-story building that moves. That starts to give you an idea of what it looks like to stand next to a bucket-wheel excavator.

As complicated and immense as the machine looks, its basic concept is really pretty simple. At the end of a long boom, there is a large wheel with buckets attached. The wheel turns the buckets into the side of mine pit, scooping up the soil and rocks, and dumping them onto a conveyor belt on the boom.

Like giant draglines, the biggest bucket-wheel excavators are designed and built specifically for open-pit mines. It takes three years to complete, but when the job is done, a giant bucket-wheel excavator can remove more than three million cubic yards of dirt a day—that's enough to fill a 20-story building. A big problem with these machines, though, is that they only work in areas with soft materials. The bucket wheels are not big enough to handle large rocks and hard ground.

Giant Bucket-Wheel Excavator at Work

1. **Undercarriage holds up and moves the machine**
2. **Superstructure houses the booms, conveyor systems, and hoisting winch**
3. **Booms hold the bucketwheel, counterweight, and conveyor system**
4. **Conveyor belts carry dirt and materials**
5. **Bucketwheel does the actual digging**
6. **Counterweight balances the bucket wheel and its boom**

'Round and 'Round

The largest bucket-wheel excavators have buckets the size of small cars. Each wheel has between 10 and 24 buckets. The harder the material being dug, the greater the number of buckets used. The boom places the wheel to remove dirt as the bucket comes up and then dumps the dirt on to a conveyor belt on the other side as the bucket goes back down.

Where are They?

Unless you visit a mine, it is very unusual to see a giant bucket-wheel excavator. Because they only work well in areas with soft soils, there are very few of them in the United States. The machines are often used in Germany where they have been digging in coal mines for more than 80 years. Others are used in mines in Africa, India, and Australia. Smaller bucket-wheel excavators, however, frequently work in docks and other places that stockpile gravel, coal, and other materials.

A Short History

The great Italian inventor Leonardo da Vinci came up with the concept of a bucket-wheel excavator 500 years ago. It wasn't until steam engines were invented, however, that the idea could become a reality. When engineers dug the Suez Canal in the 1860s, bucket-wheel excavators were used with great success in the sandy desert. When engineers used the machines to dig the Panama Canal, however, the harsh, rocky conditions proved to be too tough. In the 1930s German engineers started to develop large machines for coal mines where the excavators have been very successful. To this day, German companies build the largest bucket-wheel excavators.

Underground Mining Equipment

More than a hundred years ago, people used shovels and picks to dig mines. Beams made of wood were used to hold up the dirt and rocks. Because the mines were so narrow, children were sent inside to do the work. Those days are long over. Companies now use special equipment to dig and remove coal, gold, and other materials in hard-to-reach places. These mines can be 1,000 feet below the ground or deeper.

There are three basic jobs in underground mining. 1) Digging the dirt, rocks, coal, and other materials in the ground, 2) removing it, and 3) keeping the earth above from collapsing onto workers below. Companies have invented some very unusual machines to get these jobs done. Because mine shafts are so narrow, these machines look a bit peculiar.

1. Very hard studs and chisels knock off blocks of coal and rock

2. As the machines move forward, the fallen rocks and material are forced onto a conveyor belt

3. The machine is controlled by an attached box held by the operator

Super Digging Machines

Long-wall mining systems are very complicated machines that can dig a huge amount of coal in a short amount of time. In one month one of these machines removed a swath of coal three miles long, 840 feet wide, and 8 feet high. Super-powerful shearers with chisels attached move back and forth very quickly along the front of the mine. The shearers knock off pieces of coal that then fall onto a conveyor belt for removal. As this happens, the machine creeps forward with hydraulic supports to prevent the earth above from falling down.

Underground Train

Specially designed conveyor trains carry the coal, dirt, and other materials out of the mine. Mounted on wheels, they can be longer than 500 feet and can make sharp turns around corners.

A Very Short Car

Underground shuttle cars are long and wide, but very short in order to fit through the low ceilings of a coal mine. Shuttle cars can be as low as 28 inches off the ground, or shorter than a three-year-old child. This means that the driver has to lie down to steer the car.

Tunnel Boring Machines

Full-face tunnel boring machines, called TBMs for short, are like giant mechanical worms that dig enormous tunnels under the ground for roads, railways, and other purposes. The machines drill into the earth with a large cutter that slowly spins, cutting away at dirt and rocks that are then forced inside the machine through holes. The material falls onto conveyor belts which take it to the rear of the machine for removal. TBMs can dig tunnels as wide as a house at a rate of six feet an hour, but they only work well in certain kinds of soil, such as chalk and clay. TBMs can be as long as 1,000 feet, or five 747 jets in a row.

The Channel Tunnel between England and France underneath the English Channel was made by eleven tunnel boring machines. It took seven years to dig three parallel tunnels, which are each 31 miles long. Two of the tunnels are 25 feet wide and are used for trains. The other tunnel, only 16 feet wide, is used for emergencies and work crews. Most of the tunnel is more than 150 feet below the ocean floor.

In 1991 in England, two tunnels were excavated in almost the exact same conditions—one by a TBM, the other by boom-type cutterheads. The TBM excavated a tunnel at a rate of 330 feet a week, or twice as fast as the smaller cutterheads. The cutterheads, however, were put into action much more quickly and cost much less money. Engineers decided that it makes sense (and costs less) to use TBMs for tunnels longer than half a mile, and to use cutterheads for smaller projects.

A Giant Dirt Grinder

The face of a TBM, called the cutterhead, is armed with steel chisels and discs. The head spins around at a rate of three to eight times a minute, forcing the dirt and rocks into holes. Cutterheads can be as wide as 36 feet.

Stronger Arches

Did you ever wonder why tunnels have arched walls instead of square ones like in a house? The reason is simple. A rounded shape is much stronger and better able to hold up the earth than a square shape. You can see for yourself by taking two pieces of light cardboard and making two different types of tunnels. One should have an arched top and the other a rectangular one. Then place an item on top of each tunnel, such as a small piece of fruit, and see which tunnel is stronger.

Ramming Forward

This 35-foot-wide TBM has not yet been armed with chisels and picks. You can see the giant hydraulic rams toward the back that are used to force the machine forward. The rams push off from a concrete and steel lining that workers install in back of the machine.

1. Cutterhead digs into the ground like a giant drill

2. Archimedes screw forces the material into the back of the machine

3. The machine operator uses laser beams and closed-circuit television to steer the machine

4. Conveyor belts carry the material to the rear

5. Giant cement segments help hold the tunnel up and are used by the TBM to push off from

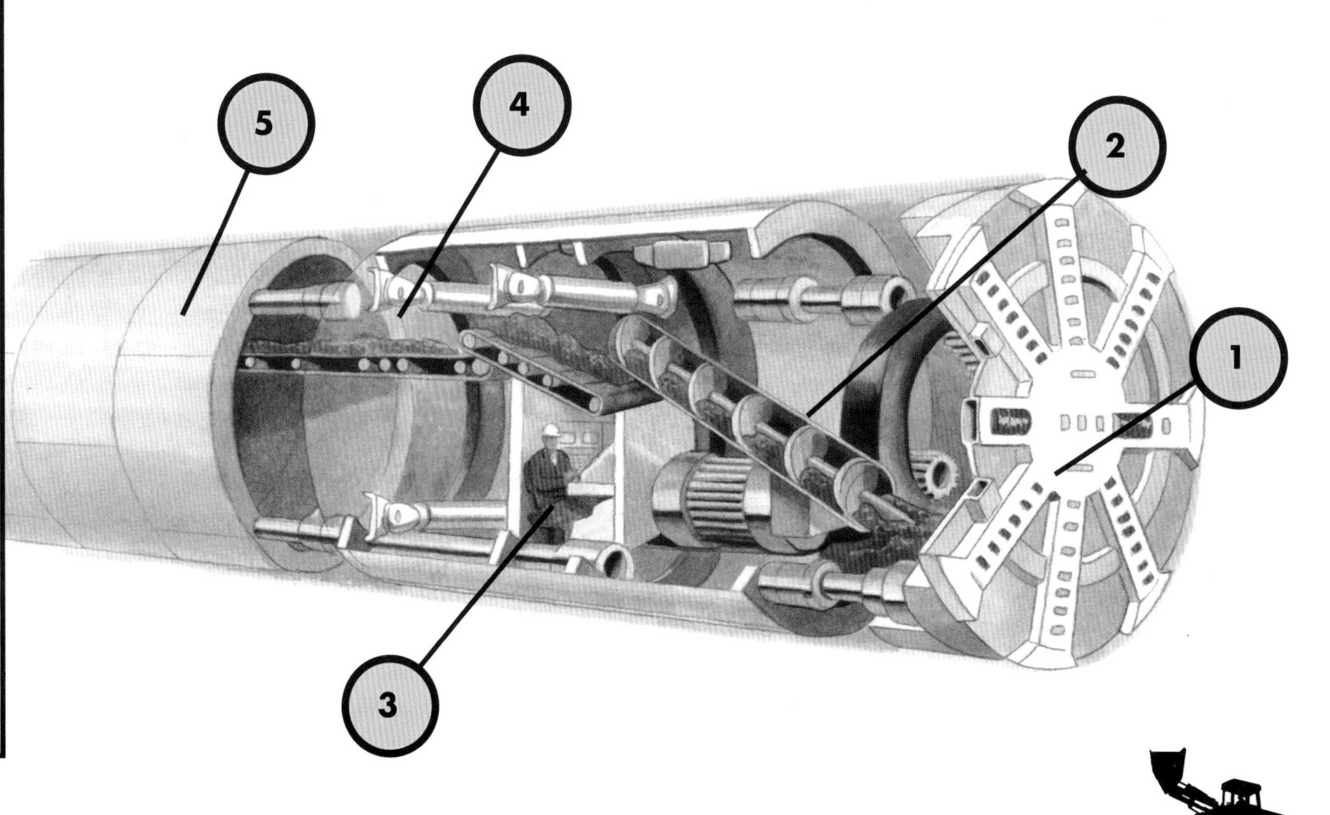

Oil Drills

Most of the oil in the world is under the ground. To reach it you have to dig holes. If you have ever tried to dig a hole in the ground, you know how much work it takes to do the job with a shovel. Drills are a much better way to reach the oil, which can then be pulled up from underneath the ground with pipes. The process is a little bit like drilling a hole in the ice on a lake and then sucking up the water below with a straw.

Of course, it's more complicated than that, especially for offshore oil rigs. Most oil wells are dug by a rotary method in which an engine turns a cluster of pipes with a large drill bit at the end. As the drill goes into the ground, the grooves push up the dirt and the pipes are put into position to draw out the oil. Some oil drills go as deep as five miles under the ground.

The most impressive oil drills are offshore platform rigs. Located in the ocean, they have to be big enough to withstand ocean storms, securely hold the oil drills, and house workers who live on the platform for weeks or months at a time. The Gullfaks "C" oil rig in the North Sea near Norway is the largest oil platform in the world. Secured to the ocean floor 108 miles from land, it rises 164 feet above the water (taller than the Eiffel Tower), holds a helipad, several large cranes, and houses a crew of 330 workers.

The first offshore drills were on converted ships anchored to the ocean floor. But even the heaviest anchors cannot keep a boat solidly in place, so new permanent oil rigs were invented. Building an offshore oil platform for deep water is a complicated and massive undertaking. There are several steps involved.

1) In a dry dock, a work area near the ocean that can be filled with water, a base is built with a series of hollow cement containers called caissons. 2) The dock is floated and the base is towed into shallow water. 3) The caissons are slowly submerged by filling them with water. 4) Concrete pillars are built on top of the caissons. 5) A platform is built on top of the pillars. 6) Pumps discharge some of the water in the caissons, allowing a tug boat to pull it into position. 7) Water refills the caissons as the platform sinks into its final position.

Turning the Screw

Instead of trying to lift a heavy object straight up it is usually easier to push or pull it up a ramp. Drills and screws are like skinny poles with spiral ramps going all the way around them. As the drill turns and presses into the ground, dirt is forced onto the ramp. As the drill goes deeper and deeper into the ground, the dirt keeps getting pushed up the drill's ramp until it comes off the drill at the top. When you use a screwdriver to press a screw into the wood the same thing happens.

Drilling the Old-Fashioned Way

The first successful oil drill was built in 1859 by Edwin Drake in a small town called Titusville in western Pennsylvania. At the time, oil was a very rare product. It cost $2 a gallon—about the same as $50 today—and was used for lamps and as a machine lubricant. Whale fat provided most of the oil in the country for lamps. Drake, whose previous job was as a train conductor, used a six-horsepower steam engine and drilling equipment built for salt wells to drill for oil. Groundwater kept flooding the drill, so he placed the drill inside a 32-foot-long pipe. After weeks of drilling, Drake struck oil 69 feet under the ground. The first oil well produced 10 to 20 barrels of oil a day, doubling the national production. But two months later, fire destroyed the wooden rig.

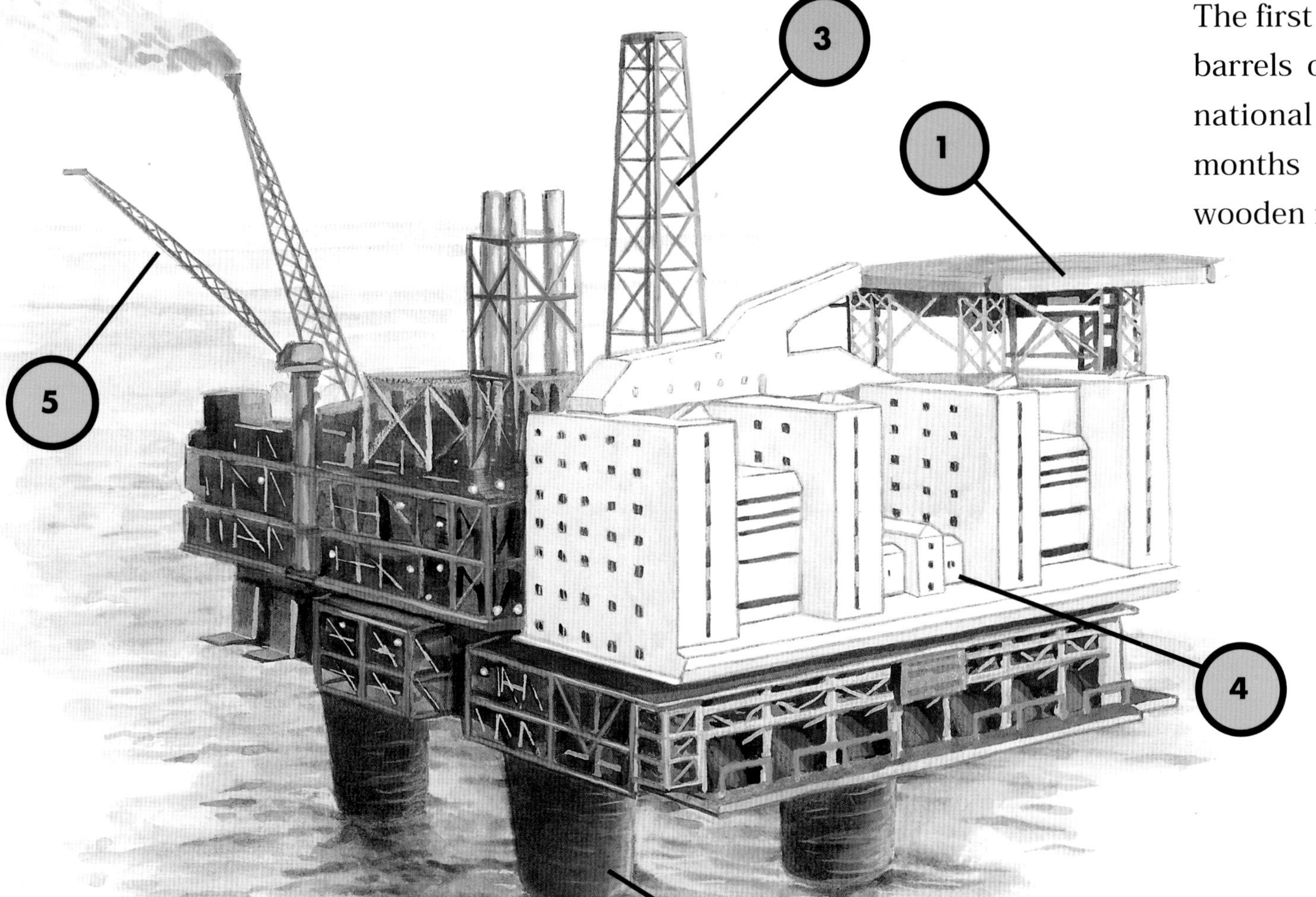

1. **Helipad**
2. **Concrete pillars**
3. **Drilling tower**
4. **Housing quarters**
5. **Pedestal cranes**

Tractors

Tractors are very important to today's farmers. Before there were tractors, people used horses and oxen to plow fields and harvest crops. Today, tractors can do all of these jobs and more. Special attachments let the tractor plow, till, cultivate, fertilize, spray, seed, forage, harvest, rake, and mow fields—all while the farmer sits inside an air-conditioned cab with a laptop computer. Tractors can also lift and drag heavy objects, tow large trailers, and travel through the toughest conditions. All of which makes a tractor the most important piece of machinery on a farm.

Plowed, Planted and Prepared to Grow

In 1837, the American blacksmith John Deere invented the first steel plow. More than 150 years later, Deere's company continues to be on the cutting edge of tractor attachments. The company's "no-till drill" carves a narrow trench as the tractor pulls it through a field. At the same time, a special machine drops seeds into the trench as a wheel behind it presses into the soil. A second wheel then crumbles the soil so that it falls on top of the seed.

Twelve-Foot Tall Tractors

The largest tractors have engines as powerful as 500 horses, weigh more than 40,000 pounds, and are up to 12 feet tall. These tractors are so heavy they need extra wheels to spread the weight so dirt does not get squashed too much. When the ground is pressed by a heavy weight, it is very difficult for plants to grow. (That's why people are not allowed to walk on the grass in some parks or gardens.) The tires are placed far apart with high axles so the tractor can drive over and between rows of plants.

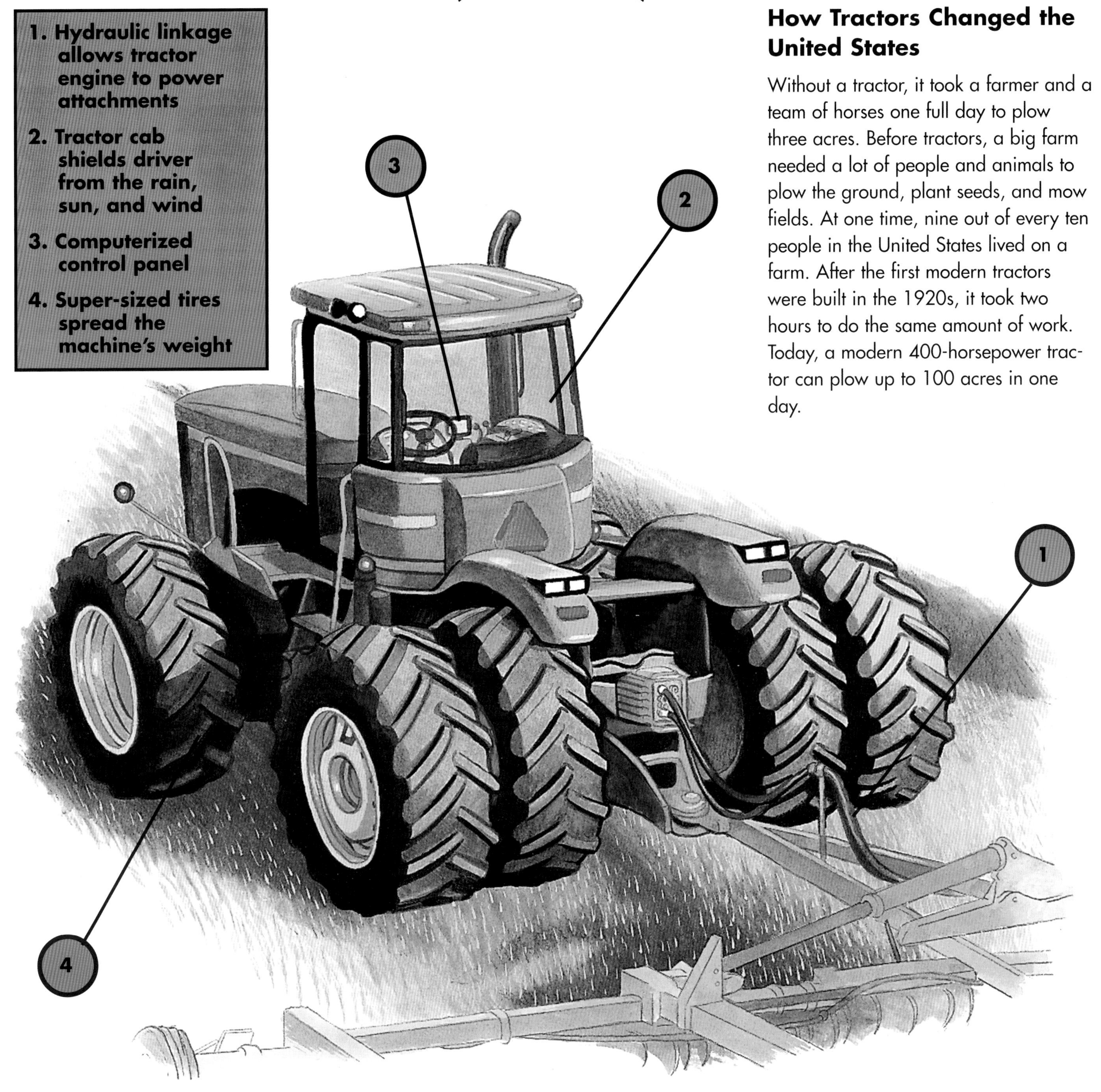

How Tractors Changed the United States

Without a tractor, it took a farmer and a team of horses one full day to plow three acres. Before tractors, a big farm needed a lot of people and animals to plow the ground, plant seeds, and mow fields. At one time, nine out of every ten people in the United States lived on a farm. After the first modern tractors were built in the 1920s, it took two hours to do the same amount of work. Today, a modern 400-horsepower tractor can plow up to 100 acres in one day.

Combine Harvester

Before there were combine harvesters, a farmer at harvest time had to cut his crop, knock the grain loose from the stalk, and then separate the grain. It took a lot of time and a lot of people. A combine harvester lets the farmer do all of those jobs with one machine. It "combines" the many tasks involved in harvesting a crop.

Combine harvesters are used for wheat, corn, peas, cotton, grass, beans, sunflowers, and other types of crops. Sometimes combine harvesters work in teams called harvest brigades to speed up the amount of time it takes to harvest many fields of crops. The largest combine harvester, which can be as powerful as 300 horses, can harvest a wheat field as large as five football fields in one hour.

Crop Flow

Champion Chomper

1. A feeder, which can be as long as 30 feet, cuts the crop with scissor-like blades and then carries it into the machine.
2. A rotating cylinder churns the crop, cutting and crushing it so that the smaller, heavier grain (or corn, peas, beans, etc.) falls through a metal grid into a grain pan. The straw (which still has some grain in it) is lifted by the cylinder onto a straw walker.
3. The straw walker looks a little bit like a crooked staircase made of metal grids. Its different parts move back and forth so that the leftover grain is shaken off the straw. As the grain falls into a pan below the straw keeps moving up the machine until it is pushed out the back of the harvester.
4. The grain in the pans is carried through the harvester with the small pieces of broken straw called chaff that also fell into the pans. A very strong fan blows the chaff out the side of the harvester.
5. Now completely separated from the straw and chaff, the grain is carried to the grain tank above the harvester where the grain spout blows it out and onto a trailer.

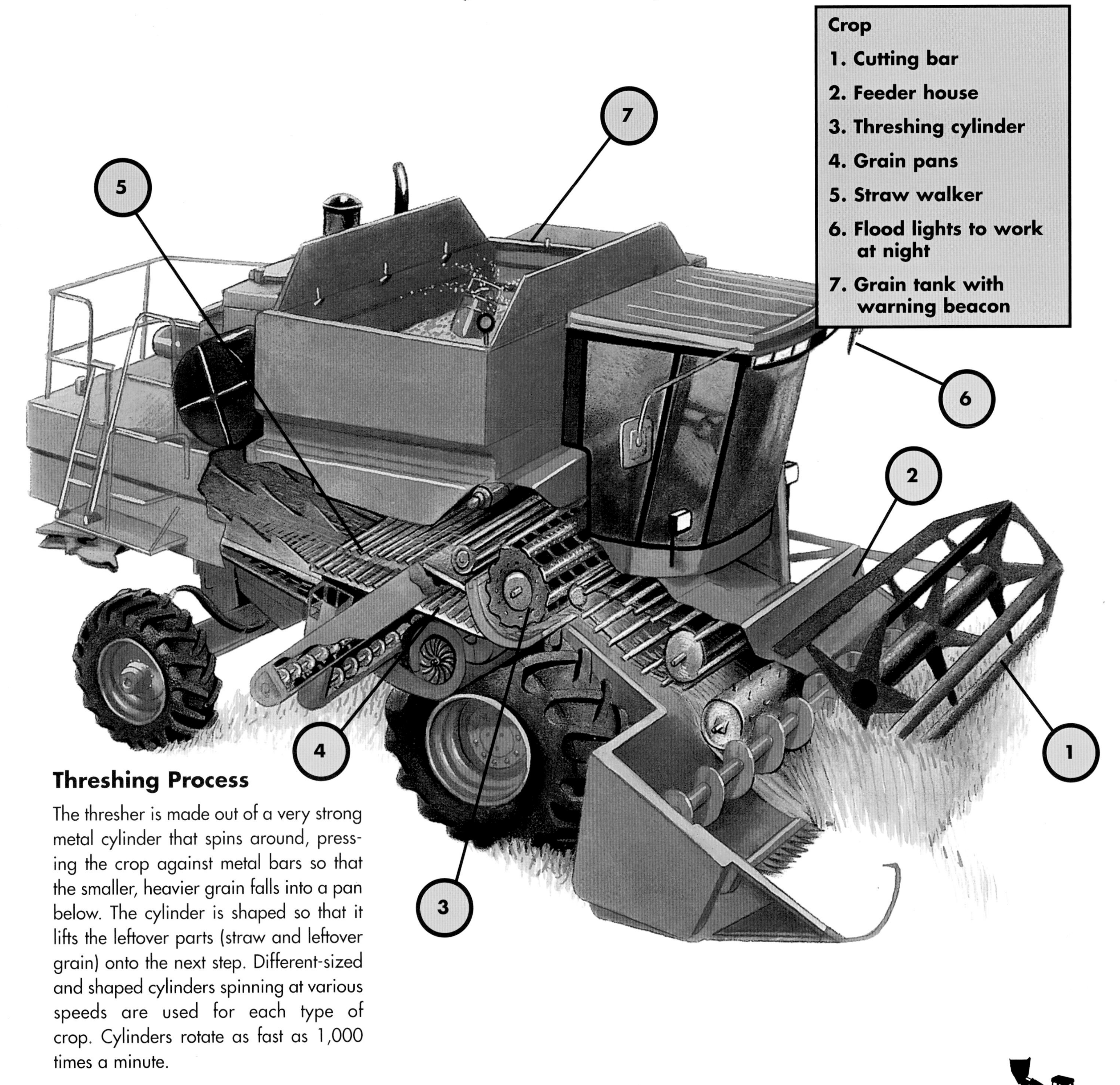

Threshing Process

The thresher is made out of a very strong metal cylinder that spins around, pressing the crop against metal bars so that the smaller, heavier grain falls into a pan below. The cylinder is shaped so that it lifts the leftover parts (straw and leftover grain) onto the next step. Different-sized and shaped cylinders spinning at various speeds are used for each type of crop. Cylinders rotate as fast as 1,000 times a minute.

Forestry Equipment

Loggers use special equipment to quickly cut trees down in ways that limit environmental damage to the forest. One of the most impressive pieces of forestry equipment is a tree harvester. It has a hydraulic arm similar to an excavator, and a harvesting head armed with saws, grips, and debarkers—sharp blades that strip bark from the tree.

The operator positions the head at the base of the tree with grippers grasping the base. A saw cuts the tree at the base and then lifts it into the air. The machine then pulls the tree through the harvesting head and the saws and debarkers remove limbs and bark. Another saw cuts the trunk into logs and they fall to the ground.

It takes the harvester less than 30 seconds to slice and dice an 80-foot tree and turn it into one pile of usable logs and another of branches and brush. Another machine, called a forwarder, then arrives to pick up the logs and carry them out of the forest. A forwarder is like a special type of tractor specially designed to drive on steep hills, around trees, and through mud. By using a tree harvester and a forwarder, loggers can cut trees in the forest without damaging other nearby trees.

Skidders

Skidders are machines designed to pick up and move tree trunks in the forest. They are sort of a cross between a tractor, a grapple, and a bulldozer. Designed to maneuver through tight corners and rough ground, skidders are one of the most common pieces of heavy equipment used by loggers.

Tree Replanting

Just as gardeners transplant flowers in a backyard, a giant tree spade removes trees by digging huge scoops of dirt underneath it and lifting the whole tree with its roots. This allows the tree to be replanted somewhere else. The biggest tree spades weigh more than 20,000 pounds. Forming a circle with six-foot-long spades, they dig deep balls of dirt around the tree and then lift it with powerful hydraulic arms.

Chipping Away

The biggest tree chippers can take a 100-foot tree and turn it into a pile of wood chips in less than a minute. With spinning knives inside the machine, tree chippers chop tree trunks, limbs, and brush into wood chips.

Some tree chippers are placed on tractor-crawlers and go directly into the woods to do their work. These are called self-propelled tree chippers. They usually have a grapple that grabs and positions trees for chipping. The wood chips are used for many different purposes, including mulch, making paper, providing fuel for wood-fired plants, and making pressed boards.

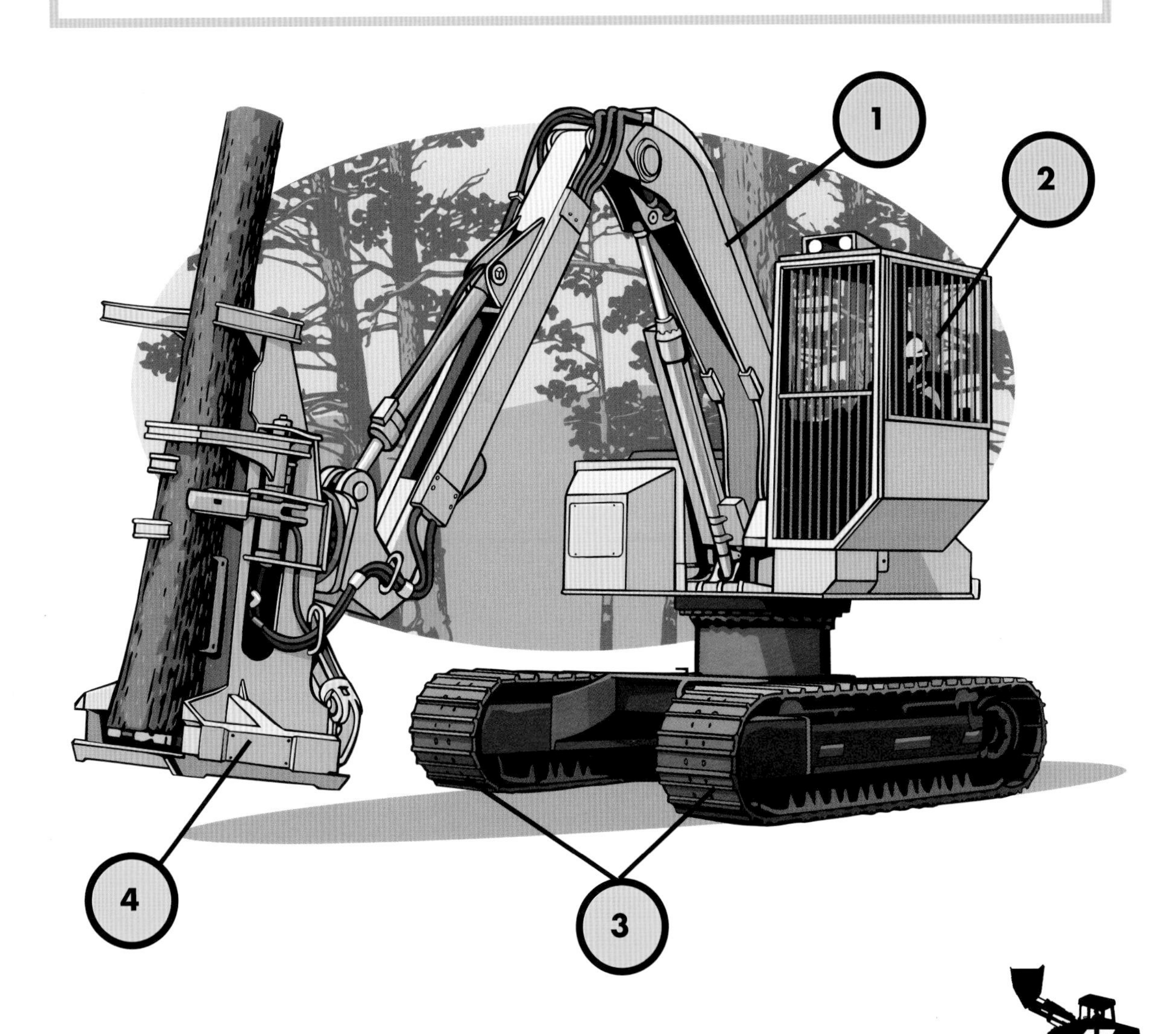

Tree Harvester Head Grips and Cuts Tree

1. **Hydraulic arm**
2. **Elevated operator's cabin for good visibility**
3. **Crawler tracks reduce soil compaction**
4. **Harvester Head**

Fire Engines

A fire engine is one of the most complex trucks built. It has to do many jobs. A fire truck has a complicated pump system that links to fire hydrants or other nearby water sources. The flow of water coming out of hoses is controlled by firefighters with the truck's pumping system. Water can pump out of hoses as fast as 1,200 gallons a minute—the equivalent of 200 cans of soda per second!

Many fire engines carry hydraulic booms or ladders to reach tall buildings. They also hold all sorts of emergency equipment, including hoses, first aid kits, uniforms, air tanks, ladders, axes, and extra nozzles and hose attachments. They have to be fast enough to drive quickly to fires, tough enough to go over rough ground in emergency situations, and sturdy enough to provide a base for powerful hoses and the hydraulic boom. Many fire trucks have hydraulic jacks attached to keep the fire engine level while the boom or ladder is in use.

Water Tank on Wheels

The primary purpose of some fire trucks is to carry water. These trucks, called pumpers, hold enough water to put out small fires. The fire truck on the left is a pumper. Hoses are attached to the back and water is pumped out to put out the flames. For larger fires, however, firefighters either need additional trucks with water to put out the blaze or find a water source nearby. This is why cities have fire hydrants. Firefighters can also use nearby lakes, rivers, or swimming pools.

Elevated Fire Fighting

The largest fire trucks carry extendable ladders or large hydraulic booms to lift firefighters high into the air. The longest booms can reach more than 200 feet high, or about as tall as a 20-story building. Some fire trucks have built-in water hoses that go along the length of the boom. Ladders on trucks sit on a revolving base called a turntable that helps position firefighters to put out the flames.

Out of the Frying Pan . . .

Firefighters wear special equipment when they fight fires. Uniforms and boots are made of special fire- and heat-resistant materials to protect the firefighters from the flames. Special face masks and visors protect their heads from flames and also protect their eyes from blinding smoke. Air tanks are strapped to their backs so that they can breathe without choking on smoke.

Water hoses are so powerful that they may require at least two people to hold and direct them. Firefighters often have to bring axes and other special equipment with them into burning houses to get through walls and closed doors.

Cement Mixers

A cement mixer truck has two basic jobs. The first job is to mix together sand, gravel, cement mix, and water to make wet cement. The other is to transport the wet cement from one place to another. A heavy, spinning tub does the mixing, while the truck does the moving.

If the mixer is spinning fast, then the dry ingredients—sand, gravel, and cement mix—are being mixed together prior to adding water. After the water is added, the mixer spins more slowly. The sloshing water can make the truck unstable, which is why a cement mixer truck usually drives slowly and has a very wide, heavy base.

All of the ingredients of wet cement are heavy, which means the truck has to have a big engine. Some cement trucks have two engines, one for driving and the other for mixing.

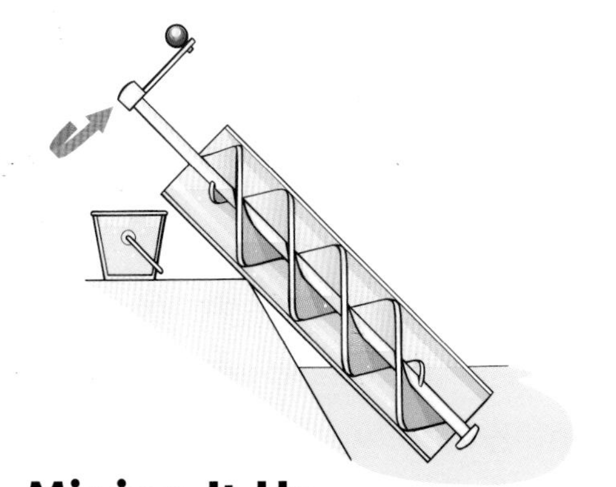

Mixing It Up

The Archmides screw was invented more than 2,000 years ago by the Greek scientist Archimedes. It is used in many machines, including tunnel boring machines, to move materials without having to push or pull. When you place a screw-like mechanism—called an auger—inside a tube and drop one end into the water, turning the screw forces water up the tube.

The inside of a cement mixer drum has a similar mechanism, except the central core has been removed. Spiraling ramps—called paddles or flights—line the inside of the drum. As the drum spins, so do the ramps. Depending on which way it turns, the cement is either pushed up or down the flights. When mixing the concrete, the drum spins the mixture down to the bottom. To pour the cement out to the delivery chute at the top, the drum turns in the opposite direction.

Ins and Outs of Cement Mixing

The dry materials for cement are placed in the drum through the hopper—the large open funnel at the top of the drum. Water is then pumped into the drum from the water tank at the other end. The dry ingredients are often mixed together first before adding the water.

While mixing the ingredients, the drum turns in one direction. But when it is time to pour the concrete, it turns in the opposite direction, forcing the cement up and into the delivery chute—a long steel tube. The chute is positioned so that the cement flows to where it is needed. After the drum is emptied, the inside has to be cleaned to prevent the cement from hardening. Water from the tank on the back of the truck is pumped into the rotating drum to wash out the inside. The water is then pumped out.

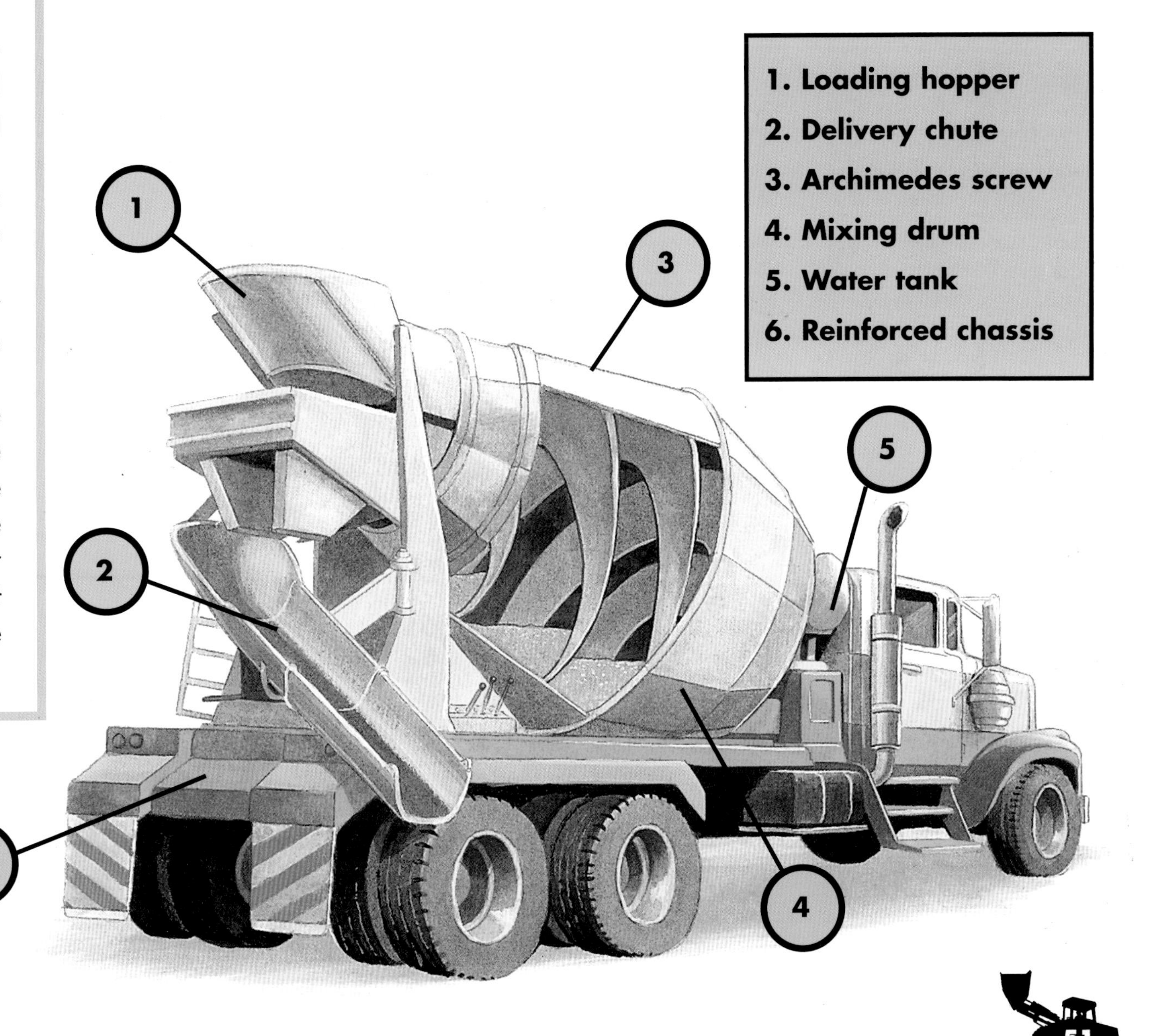

1. Loading hopper
2. Delivery chute
3. Archimedes screw
4. Mixing drum
5. Water tank
6. Reinforced chassis

Working Boats

Boats have many uses. While most are used for transportation and pleasure, some do very specific tasks. Icebreakers perform one of the most difficult jobs—breaking through ice as thick as six feet to make channels for other ships to travel through.

An icebreaker boasts a powerful engine and giant propellers at both the front and back of the boat. The hull is made out of extra-thick steel and is designed to cut through the ice. The front of the boat-called the bow-is narrow and acts like a giant knife cracking the ice.

The main body of the icebreakder is wider and heavier than most boats of similar length. The added weight helps crush the ice and the extra width allows the icebreaker to clear a wide passage.

Tugging Along

Tugboats are small powerful ships that push or pull other ships. Small enough to get around in tight areas, but strong enough to pull mighty loads, tugboats are hard-working, but not very glamorous. They can be found on rivers and oceans, tugging barges loaded with grain, oil, lumber, and other goods. They pull huge oil rigs, parts of bridges and highways, and giant pieces of equipment that are too big and bulky to be loaded onto a ship or carried over land. Tugs work in harbors all over the world, guiding massive luxury liners, cargo tankers, and other ships through narrow channels and getting them to their spaces—called berths—at the dock.

Tugboats can be as small as only 20 feet long or as large as 300 feet long. The average tugboat is about 100 feet long. The largest and most powerful tugs work on the open seas, where they are also used to save ships that have run aground or are in danger of sinking. With their powerful engines and strong tow-lines, tugboats do the kinds of simple, but essential, jobs that no other boat can.

A single river tug can push as many as 40 barges tied together and carrying 60,000 tons of cargo. A river tug can push (or pull) as much cargo as 15 railroad cars and as many as 60 tractor-trailer trucks.

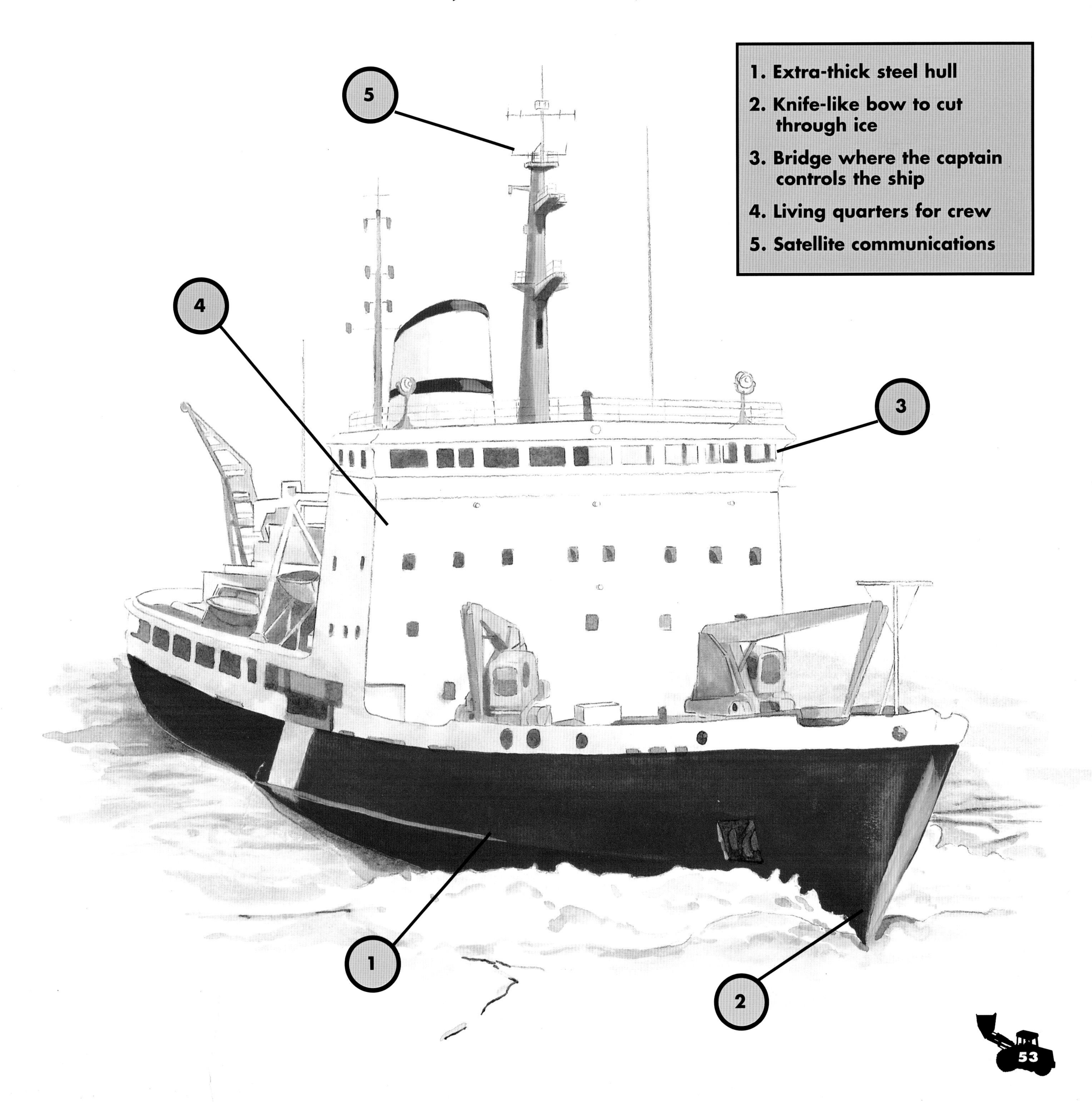
5
4
3
1
2
1. Extra-thick steel hull
2. Knife-like bow to cut through ice
3. Bridge where the captain controls the ship
4. Living quarters for crew
5. Satellite communications

Tractor-Trailer Trucks

Tractor-trailer trucks can be found on almost every highway and in every town and city. They are big, long trucks that carry materials from one place to another. There are two main parts to every tractor-trailer truck. The tractor in front holds the engine, front driving wheels, and the driver's cab. The engine is many times more powerful than a car's engine and the fuel tanks can carry 40 times more fuel than a car's gas tank. There are as many as ten tires on a truck tractor. The driver's cab often has a sleeping cabin in the rear.

The trailer holds the goods that are being transported. It is attached to the rear of the tractor. Most trailers have long rectangular metal boxes to hold the materials, but some are open to hold large pieces of equipment and others are designed to carry certain things like logs or cars.

Called a semi or a rig, a tractor-trailer truck is designed to carry heavy materials for long distances. They are typically 13 feet high and 55 feet long. Sometimes an extra trailer will be attached to the rear of the trailer to carry more materials. This is called a double semi-trailer and it can be 70 feet long. Because the truck is broken up into different parts, it can turn corners much more easily.

Cutting into the Wind

Tractor-trailer trucks push a lot of air when they drive fast. If you have ever put your hand outside a car while it is moving, you probably noticed that when you hold your hand flat and point it to the sky the wind pushes your hand back. But when you point your fingers into the wind, it is much easier to hold your hand steady because your fingers cut into wind. Because trucks are so big, they have special features to make it easier to cut through the wind.

The illustration on the right shows what an aerodynamically designed truck might look like in the future. It's aerodynamic features include rounded edges at the front of the truck, a curved collar at the top of the tractor to deflect wind before it hits the flat front of the trailer, and covered wheels with panels to provide a flat surface to reduce the drag. With these kinds of design features, the truck's engine does not have to work as hard and less fuel is needed.

1
2
7
6
3
5
4
1. Trailer
2. Sleeping cabin
3. Driver's cab
4. Large sideview mirrors
5. Extra-large fuel tank
6. Two exhaust pipes
7. Curved collar to cut the wind

Locomotives

The invention of locomotives almost 200 years ago changed the world. Able to carry people and products on land over vast distances, they helped connect towns and cities, paved the way for industrial economies, and made traveling a much simpler, faster, and more pleasant experience.

The locomotive is a big, powerful engine on wheels that pulls dozens of train cars thousands of miles. Using several locomotives connected together, a train itself can be more than a mile long, carrying everything from stacks of cars to huge shipments of grain to cartons of frozen food. Trains are especially important for hauling heavy materials such as coal, fuel, and lumber over long distances.

About 16 feet high, large locomotives range in length from 50 to 80 feet. They can weigh 425,000 pounds or more and have huge fuel tanks, which hold 6,000 gallons of diesel fuel—enough to fill 120 bathtubs. The heavy weight and large pool of fuel is needed to power the giant engine inside the locomotive; it can be as strong as 6,000 horses. The engine, which can weigh 34,000 pounds (more than 100 times the size of a car engine) turns the wheels—called the truck—on the locomotive.

1. Steam Locomotive

The first locomotives, built in the early 1800s, used steam engines. Burning wood or coal in the firebox, heated water created steam pressure inside the engine. The pressure was used to power large pistons that were connected to the locomotive's wheels. Steam locomotives were very successful for many years but they needed someone to constantly fill the firebox with wood and coal—a hot, dirty, job. Steam engines were also inefficient and needed a lot of maintenance. Steam locomotives are hardly ever used now.

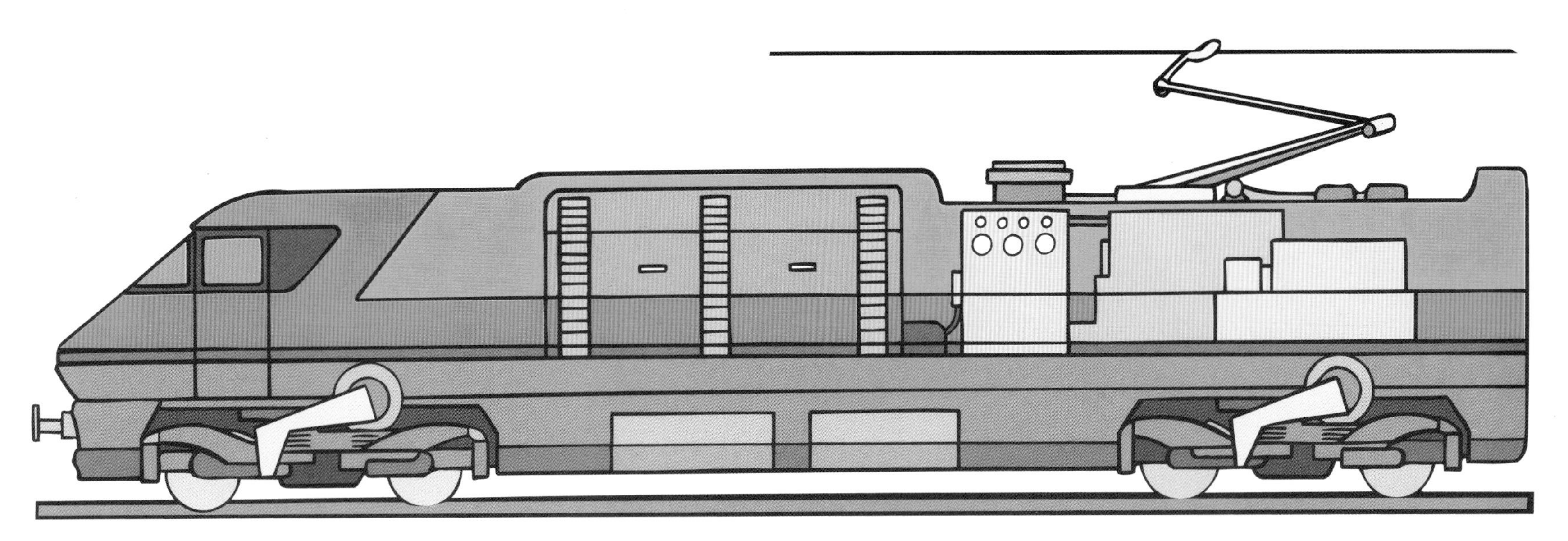

2. Electric Locomotive

Electric locomotives use electricity generated from a central electric plant to drive the locomotive's wheels. The electric current comes from either an overhead cable called a catenary, or from a third rail along the train track. The first electric train was used in 1879 in Germany. Electric locomotives are relatively quiet, efficient, easy to accelerate, and clean to operate. They are particularly useful in cities where there is a lot of train traffic and the train is often required to stop and go a lot. The fastest trains in the world, sometimes called bullet trains, are electric locomotives. The biggest problem with electric locomotives is that it is very expensive to build them.

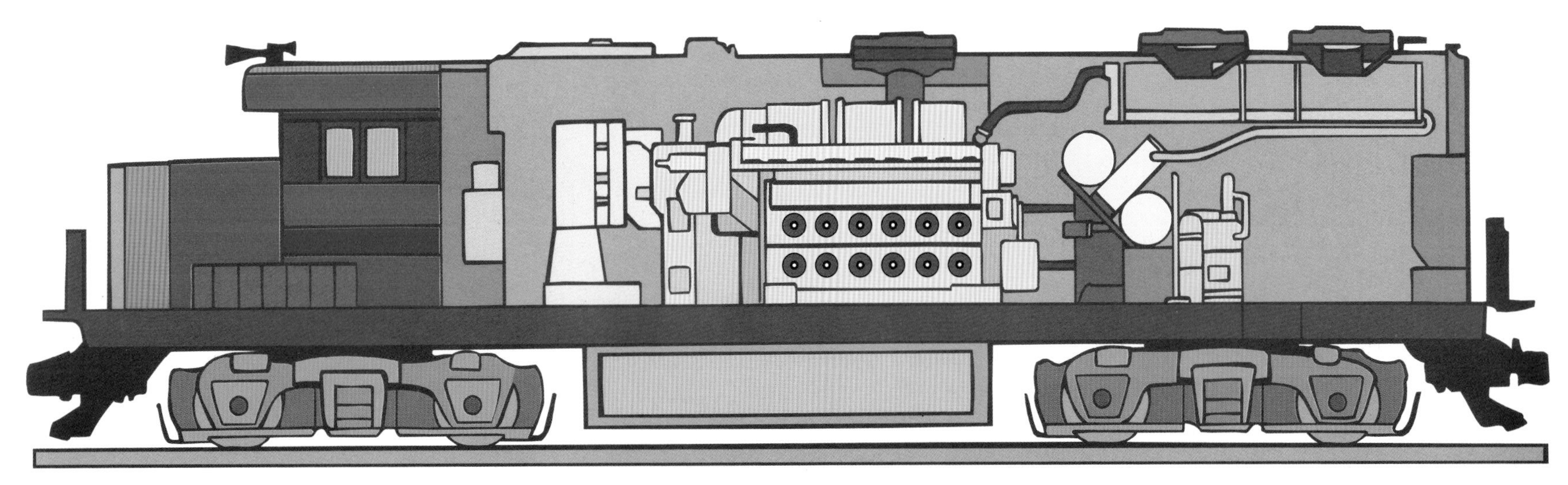

3. Diesel Locomotive

Diesel locomotives are similar to electric trains in that they use electricity to drive the wheels. The difference is that instead of drawing power from a distant source, the locomotive uses special fuel (diesel fuel) and a generator to generate electricity to move the wheels. The first diesel engine was invented by Rudolf Diesel in Germany in 1898. Diesel locomotives—also known as diesel-electric locomotives—are the most popular type of locomotive, especially in the United States where more than 95 percent of the passenger and freight trains use diesel engines.

NASA Crawler Transporter

Two of the best-known giant machines in the world are Hans and Franz, the pair of six million-pound crawler-transporters at the NASA Kennedy Space Center in Florida. The two take turns carrying space shuttles and the mobile launch pad down a special runway and positioning the spaceships for liftoff. The vehicles were built in 1965-66 by a company that built giant strip-mining shovels. Hans and Franz have each traveled more than 1,000 miles, carrying as much as 13 million pounds at a time. But these machines are about more than brute strength, they also use complicated leveling systems to perfectly position the space shuttle so it can blast off into space.

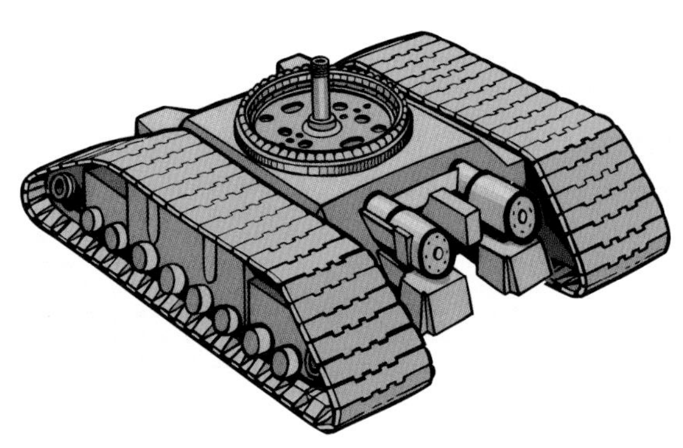

Big Feet

The crawler-transporter has four double-tracked crawlers to move it. Each one of the crawlers is 7 1/2 feet wide, 10 feet tall and 41 feet long. There are 57 shoes per track. Each shoe weighs a ton, or as much as 35 seven-year-old children. Two gigantic engines as powerful as 5,500 horses make the crawler move forward.

Special Road

NASA built a special road as wide as an eight-lane highway for the crawler-transporter to carry the Space Shuttle from the Vehicle Assembly Building to one of two launch sites 3.4 and 4.2 miles away. The machine travels less than one mile per hour and it usually takes about five hours to complete the trip. The crawler uses 150 gallons of fuel per mile, which is more than 3,000 times as much as a typical car. After the Space Shuttle takes off, it goes two miles per hour back to the Vehicle Assembly Building. This building is one of the largest in the world. The door is as tall as a 45-story building. When NASA painted an American flag on the side, they used 6,000 gallons of paint.

Three, two, one . . . blast-off!

The crawler-transporter is 131 feet long, 114 feet wide, and 20 feet tall. The deck of the mobile launch pad is about 90 feet on each side, making it the size of a baseball diamond. The deck is flat, but when it goes up a ramp, a complicated leveling system moves the deck so that the space shuttle keeps pointing straight up. There are two control cabs at each end of the machine to drive the crawlers.

Space Equipment

Heavy equipment in space really isn't very heavy. The world's first crane on the Space Shuttle weighs 902 pounds and is about as big as a telephone pole. On earth it is not even strong enough to lift its own weight. But in space, where there is no gravity and objects are weightless, it can catch and position a 65,000-pound satellite.

A new generation of space equipment is in the works for the construction and operation of the International Space Station. Like the Canadarm, this equipment has to be able to withstand the rigors of space. Light but tough materials such as titanium, stainless steel and graphite epoxy make up the components to weather the extreme fluctuations in temperature. An insulated blanket with heaters keeps the Canadarm at about zero degrees Celsius. The blanket also protects the metal from the heat of the sun's powerful rays.

Operators use computers to maneuver the equipment. Hundreds of electric wires control the movements. The amount of power needed to move these long mechanical arms is very low. The Canadarm on the space shuttle uses about the same amount of energy as an electric tea kettle. Computerized thrusters—like tiny jets—counter the impact of the arm catching and releasing objects. The space shuttle Canadarm's thrusters are precisely coordinated to keep the shuttle on course when it catches and maneuvers large satellites.

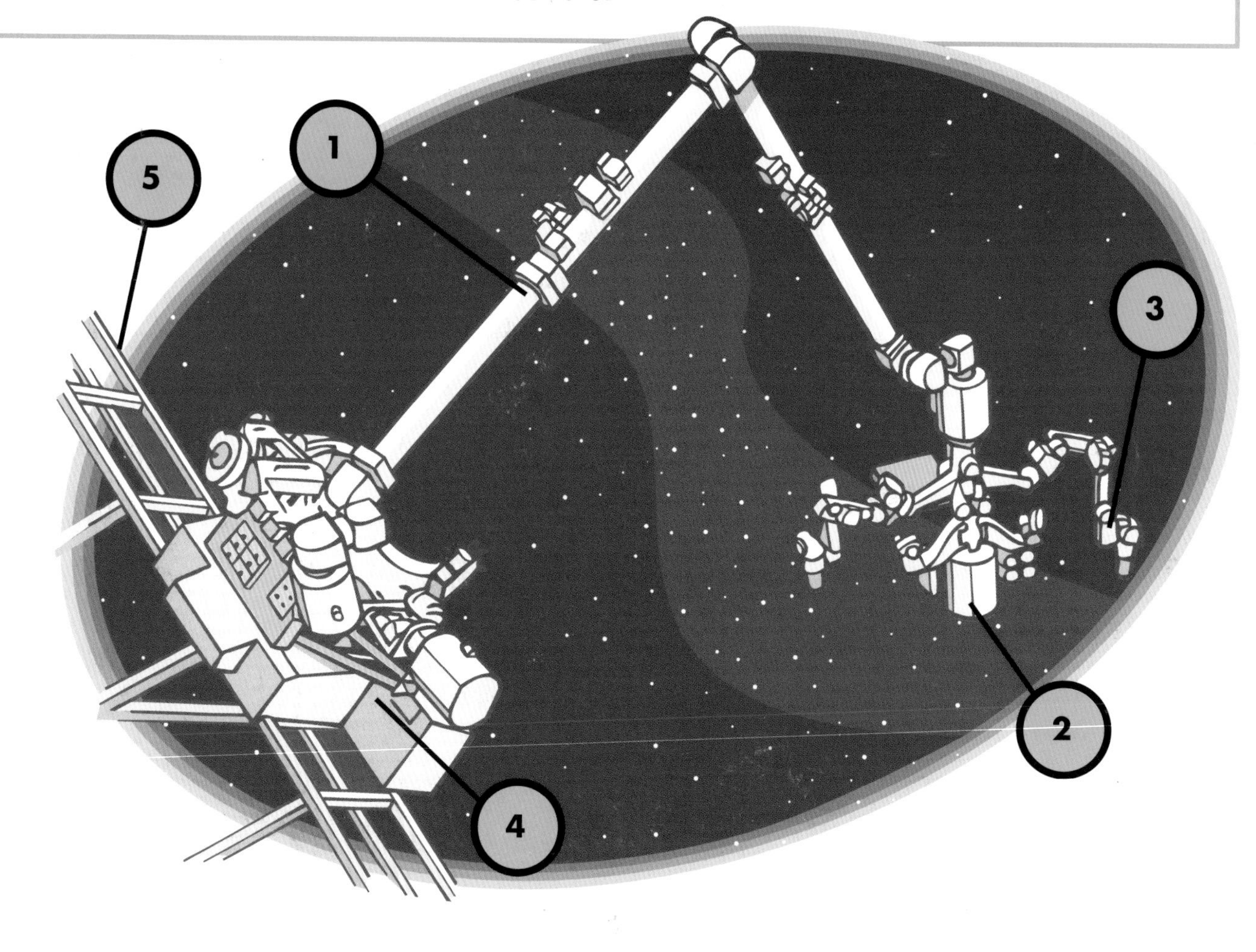

1. **Remote Manipulator System (Canadarm)**
2. **Special Purpose Dexterous Manipulator (Canada Hand)**
3. **Robotic arms**
4. **Mobile Servicer Base System**
5. **International Space Station**